THE CORNBALL
SYNDROME

THE CORNBALL SYNDROME

by

M. A. Clarke

SPANGLE PRESS
Linden, The Vale, Chalfont-St.-Peter
Buckinghamshire, England

Printed in Great Britain by
Conservation Printing
ISBN 0 9510957 0 6

WE STARVED IN AFRICA, YOU CLOSED YOUR EYES AND SAID "IT'S NOT MY PROBLEM".

WE PLEADED FOR HELP IN IRELAND, NICARAGUA AND SOUTH AFRICA, YOU CLOSED YOUR EYES AND SAID "IT'S NOT MY PROBLEM".

WE LOST OUR JOBS AND COMMUNITIES, YOU CLOSED YOUR EYES AND SAID "IT'S NOT MY PROBLEM".

WE RIOTED ON THE STREETS AGAINST BRUTALITY AND INJUSTICE, YOU CLOSED YOUR EYES AND SAID "IT'S NOT MY PROBLEM".

WE WERE IMPRISONED, BELITTLED, SLANDERED AND MISREPRESENTED, YOU CLOSED YOUR EYES AND SAID "IT'S NOT MY PROBLEM".

WE WERE BEATEN, RAPED AND HUMILIATED, YOU CLOSED YOUR EYES AND SAID "IT'S NOT MY PROBLEM".

WE STRETCHED OUT OUR ARMS TO YOU FROM PADDED CELLS, YOU CLOSED YOUR EYES AND SAID "IT'S NOT MY PROBLEM".

WE CRIED FOR MERCY WITH PITIFUL WHIMPERS FROM OUR EXPERIMENTAL CAGES AND SLAUGHTERHOUSE TERRORS, YOU CLOSED YOUR EYES AND SAID "IT'S NOT MY PROBLEM".

AND WHEN WE PROTESTED, DEMONSTRATED AND WITHDREW OUR LABOUR, YOU CLOSED YOUR EYES AND SAID "IT'S NOT MY PROBLEM".

When are you going to realize — you ARE *the problem.*

CONTENTS

Author's notes
Preface
Foreword

SECTION ONE: CORNBALL CHARACTER
1. Who are the cornballs?
2. Cornball Traditionalists
3. Cornball mythology

SECTION TWO: UPHOLDING THE STATUS QUO
1. Rich world. Poor world
2. Rich folk. Poor folk
3. A woman's place
4. All creatures great and small
5. Environmental Nemesis

SECTION THREE: THE CORNBALL ESTABLISHMENT
1. Formal Education
2. The Media
3. The Law
4. The Church

SECTION FOUR: EVERYDAY CORNBALL POLITICS
1. Unhealthy politics
2. Politics, gender and morality
3. Talking politics

SECTION FIVE: CORNBALL POWER POLITICS
1. Ideology and mythology
2. Third World Britain

SECTION SIX: CONCLUSIONS
Afterword
Post Script

AUTHOR'S NOTES

1. Every year, more and more of our precious wild life is lost to us forever. Every year our heritage of natural beauty is eroded and despoiled to produce wheat mountains for no other reason than to line the pockets of a greedy minority. Every year our landscape is further ravaged, scarred and homogenised to construct more and more motorways. Every year a staggering 175 million trees (a forest the size of Wales) are felled to supply Britain alone with its demand for paper — largely to oil the monstrous machinery of industrial capitalism and bureaucracy. Every year more and more vital third world agricultural land is desertified by unchecked deforestation in the interests of profit.

These facts are a serious indictment of a wasteful, imprudent system of conducting human affairs and of the wasteful, imprudent life styles of those throughout the industrialized world who squander our precious resources (and those of the third world) with no thought for tomorrow. In recognition of the pressing need for a frugal, responsible attitude towards the consumption of the earth's resources and for the conservation of the country's natural beauty I have therefore chosen to have this book printed on recycled paper. My arguments for the need for further measures in this direction, and my suggestions as to the nature of their implementation, appear throughout the book.

2. **SOCIALISM = 'STATE OWNERSHIP OF THE MEANS OF PRODUCTION, DISTRIBUTION AND EXCHANGE'.**

Implicit in this dictionary definition of socialism is the assumption that 'STATE' means 'GOVERNMENT' and not 'PEOPLE', since it is automatically assumed that people have to be governed to prevent them reverting to the jungle. It is important to recognise this, because it leads to a multitude of misunderstandings about what we all mean when we talk about 'socialism'.

I should make it abundantly clear at the outset, therefore, that whenever I talk about 'socialism' it should be taken to mean simply "equal access to information and services and equal apportionment of available resources (either individually or as a community or communities)", with no assumptions either about the existence of Government and centralized power or about the necessity for wealth creation, economics and material growth. If I wish to make distinctions about the various types of socialism and the varying forms of social organization they imply I will be more explicit, i.e. [1]National Socialism, Bureaucratic Socialism, Patriarchal Socialism, Authoritarian Socialism, [2]Autonomous Socialism etcetera. I hope this simplifies rather than complicates the polemic.

3. Since this book is self-published and self-edited I've no doubt it still contains quite a number of rough edges, despite my attempts to knock them off, as it is extremely difficult to make an objective appraisal of something you've been living and breathing for . . . well, a long time. I can only apologise to the literary purists for any offence caused to their sensibilities and hope that in the interests of communication they will grin and bear it.

1. I have found it necessary to draw a distinction between National Socialism and Autonomous Socialism that some people may find untenable, but my reasons for doing this were two-fold. a) In fear of any association with Hitler's doctrine, which was practised under the same name. In fact, his philosophy should more accurately have been called 'Ethnic Socialism', under which only the elite and selected few were destined for any kind of equality, since the term 'National' suggests the whole population. Also, his use of the word 'socialism' must be considered highly suspect given his pathological detestation of Marxists and his obsessional adherence to what he called 'the aristocratic principle of Nature' — but then he wasn't noted for his logic. All this, however, does not make me feel any easier with the term and I would prefer to divorce myself from it entirely. b) National Socialism is not, of necessity, built on National self-sufficiency and could easily be dependent on foreign trade and foreign investments (both domestic and external) — nor does it necessarily allow for individual autonomy and could be run by a minority in a centralized power structure. (Although realistically it should then be called 'Authoritarian Socialism', which just proves how ambiguous the term can be). It is important to bear in mind that National Socialism built on wealth creation becomes international capitalism and merely shifts the burden of exploitation from one set of people to another — albeit a bit further away.

2. I believe some Anarchists may find my philosophy plagiaristically re-named 'Autonomous Socialism' and for this I apologise. However, the term 'Anarchist' has acquired a number of connotations over the years that I am not prepared to associate myself with, nor do I believe that all those at present using the word are entirely in agreement about what it means to them. To me the term 'right-wing Anarchist' is totally meaningless.

4. I would like to express my thanks to the following for permission to print extracts:—

1. Longman Publishers for 'Roget's Thesaurus'
2. Penguin Books for 'The Jungle' by Upton Sinclair, © Upton Sinclair
3. Centaur Press for 'Food for a Future' by Jon Wynne-Tyson
4. Marion Boyars for 'Limits to Medicine' by Ivan Illich

and to acknowledge 'Los Viejos' by Grace Halsell and 'Only one Earth' by Barbara Ward and René Dubos as having influenced some of the thoughts expressed in the book. A special thank you to Jon Wynne-Tyson for his friendly advice and illuminating insights into the world of publishing.

I would also like to extend my gratitude to Mick Jenson of White Space Studios both for his help and for his work on the book jacket, to Sophie Dickson for her illustrations and to Charles Clarke Printers for their friendly and helpful treatment of a struggling first-time publisher.

Above all, my very special thanks to Pat Lester for . . . everything.

PREFACE

☆ The patriarchal status quo presents women with the problem of how to overcome the inequality and oppression caused to them by men

☆ The centralist status quo presents both men and women with the problem of how to overcome the inequality and oppression caused to the majority by a powerful minority

☆ The capitalist status quo, coupled with national wealth creation and unchecked industrial growth, presents us all with problems of pollution, environmental destruction and third world exploitation.

These are the pillars, in various permutations, on which 20th century societies the world over are founded, and the problems they present constitute the malaise of the human condition. Undeniably, each contributes its own distinctive forms of aggravation, but they should not be approached in isolation because solutions achieved in this way will not, eventually, prove satisfactory. Abolition of the patriarchal status quo without abolition of capitalism would mean living in a competitive, cut-throat society in which women, of necessity, would be forced to subordinate their child-bearing and suckling roles — the last area in which man still has to bow his head in acknowledgement of a power greater than himself, in which woman still feels the mystical connection of her body with her soul and in which God and Nature are still united — in deference to the [1]'productive' priorities of economics. Her gender would finally disappear in test tube reproduction, genetic engineering and bottle feeding. Neutered, she would finally be man's equal — a genderless, soul-less production unit in a mechanical, soul-less, materialistic world. Similarly, abolishing capitalism without altering the present state of male dominance (centred around the assumed superiority

---

1. *'Productive' meaning the production of excess for trade and profit rather than for subsistence and the meeting of actual needs.*

of masculine, over feminine, values) and male-male competition for the favours (and services) of subjugated women would lead inexorably to a centralized, militaristic, chauvinistic state bent on warmongering expansionism and encompassing inequality and individual repression. Abolition (on a national basis) of both capitalism AND the patriarchy would not, of necessity, save the environment from destruction because *matriarchal* (or genderless) Authoritarian Socialism could just as easily be built on national wealth creation and economic growth as *patriarchal* socialism. Unless the need for economic expansion and consumer societies is reviewed (together with the social indoctrination necessary to propel the individual towards them) then the environment will continue to be abused and the need for centralized power structures with built-in social controls against the abuse of artificially-created scarcities will continue to appear indispensable. Attitudes, as well as power structures, have to be challenged. Materialism is just as much a curse of the 20th century as the patriarchy, capitalism and centralized power — and probably singly the most damaging factor of all to the overall joy of living.

In order to change society — and ourselves — for the better, we must open our eyes beyond the warp and weft, and see the whole *fabric* set out before us. The private car causes pollution, death, environmental destruction and increasingly restricted mobility — all of which are undesirable. To abolish it in favour of public transport, however, necessarily means a head-on collision with the free-market economy and industrial expansion. It is naive, therefore, to imagine that it is possible to be a conservationist and an industrial capitalist simultaneously. Territorial aggression and a thirst for dominance are the masculine attributes which have always led us into bloody and ridiculous wars and which are at present threatening to destroy us all. It is contradictory and short-sighted, therefore, to join CND while refusing to support women's fight to alter male priorities. It is often assumed that animal rights campaigners have little relevance to, or connection with, the unacceptable nature of capitalism, the problems of the third world or the struggles of feminists — but decimating forests and growing crops in order to feed livestock destined for rich-world meat eaters causes hardship and starvation in third world countries; animals die in their thousands for the profits to be made from Ivory and fur coats; and little boys who are 'soft' about animals are likely to be chastised, derided . . . and branded with the dreaded insult 'cissy'.

This book is about connections — and about attitudes. It is about seeing the association between attitudes, individual actions, personal unhappiness and the problems of the world. It is about the unacceptable nature of the present status quo and about the people — *the cornballs* — whose attitudes are largely responsible for its continuation. It is an angry protest against a society that applauds selfishness and rewards greed; that awards knighthoods and titles to anybody who, either through inheritance or by single-minded, ruthless exploitation of the weak, the unfortunate and the powerless, accumulates vast amounts of the resources that should, in the name of any God worthy of the name, be used to enhance the lives of ALL humankind equally. It is an emphatic rejection of a twisted set of values that deems 'successful' anybody who controls and suppresses their human instinct for compassion in order to take advantage of any opportunity to get rich at the expense of the lives and happiness of as many people as the task requires. It is a gesture of disgust against those who bow in homage to the owners of flash, expensive cars and blood-soaked fur coats — to anybody, in effect, wallowing in excesses of every kind — while reserving their most scathing contempt for life's losers — the poor, the powerless, the petty criminal, the victim. It is an impassioned plea to all those who care about our ravaged world and the majority of its ill-used inhabitants to take action against the new 'realism' that insists we must turn our backs on the weak, the needy and the starving, close our eyes to the earth's anguish and our ears to the rising crescendo of cries for help. It is written as an expression of solidarity with all those who spend the greater part of their waking hours hammering against a brick wall of cornball ignorance and intransigence and as a gesture of commiseration with all those who suffer, day in, day out, from the effects of cornball greed, selfishness and prejudice. Finally, it is an appeal to the young — in whose hands the fate of the planet and its inhabitants ultimately rests — to use their energy, their idealism and their imagination in the pursuit of creating a better, saner society . . . a society in which cornballs and their unsavoury attitudes no longer exist.

FOREWORD

As a prologue I would like to address the following questions to the cornballs out there and hope that by the end of the book (supposing any get that far) they have come up with some answers:—

If you are so concerned about blacks and aliens crowding out your culture, why do you continue to support the system that drives them here from their native lands to escape their colonial-induced poverty?

If you are so concerned about foreigners "coming over here, taking our jobs and houses and living off the backs of the British people" then why do you happily allow foreign business interests to move in here with their foreign directors and foreign parent-companies to exhaust your precious and rapidly diminishing resources, to dictate the terms of your employment and to use your labour to line their own pockets? Why, when so many British people are homeless and destitute are you not concerned that the families of foreign company directors rent sumptuous, five-bedroomed houses in London and the suburbs and make it virtually impossible for most homeless families to find reasonably priced rented accommodation? Why do you cheerfully buy Japanese radios, American cars and French apples which destroys British industry and puts our own British workers on the dole? Why are you so unperturbed at the spectacle of rich tourists from America, Australia and South Africa living off the fat of the land in 5-star hotels, taking home the fruits of British labour in luxury items, using all the facilities that the country has to offer and treating British workers like their personal servants — while your own compatriots live in poverty all around you?

If you are so concerned to be 'British' and to maintain your freedom and sovereign identity, why do you happily allow yourself to be increasingly dominated by American culture, have your precious land occupied by American bases (via NATO) and your life dictated by American capital?

Do you not consider that your anger towards the impoverished British black on the dole queue and the housing list may not be, if not misguided, at least misdirected?

SECTION ONE

CORNBALL CHARACTER

CORNBALL . . . straight, conformer, toer-of-the-line, teacher's pet, toady, sneak, approval-seeker, yes-kid, young fogey, punk-hater, hippy-hater, black-hater, paki-basher, queer-basher, scab, informer, kow tower, snob, cap-doffer, groveller, rich man's lackey, women's lib hater, sexist pig, slob, Irish-joke-teller, sorry-to-be-sexist-but. . . bore, money grubber, grasper, status seeker, human nature quoter, middle-of-the roader, prig, hypocrite, prude, old fogey, brown rice knocker, health freak sniggerer, anti vegetarian, anti animal rights, anti ecology movement, anti left wing, anti progressive thought, anti political discussion, anti controversial subjects, anti making waves, anti thought of any kind, anti protest movements, anti upsetting the dinner party with provocative ideas, pro police, pro army, pro nuclear, pro stricter discipline, pro lots and lots of punishment, pro short sharp shocks, pro public schools, pro private health care for the rich, anti union, anti strike, anti equality, Sun reader, yah, yuppy, yumpy, image seeker, fast car lover, engine revver, striver, fawner, hanger on, sucker up, promotion seeker, worshipper of the rich, Les Dawson fan, establishment stooge, upper class twit, brayer, chinless wonder, pain in the ass.

1. WHO ARE THE CORNBALLS?

The people who are to form the central subject matter in these pages will be recognizable to just about everybody, since they are not altogether uncommon. Cornball Petes, Olivers, Henries and Jeans can be found in any office, factory and shop and behind the net curtains of any Close or Crescent in the country. Whereas in numbers they do not form a majority of the population they are nonetheless represented by extremely powerful minorities the world over. Their influence is therefore ominously widespread and, tragically, it is their beliefs, their values and their prejudices that dominate all our lives. They do not come exclusively from any one section of the community, but they all have certain things in common and are easy to identify. Their reading matter, for example, is limited to *The Sun, The Telegraph, The Times, The Mail, The Express* and *The Star* in the week and *The People, The News of the World* and *The Sunday Times* (et al) on the Sabbath. No cornball worthy of the name would be caught reading *The Guardian* and most would ban *The Socialist Worker* on the grounds of subversion. *City Limits* is a definite no-no to respectable London cornballs and the ideas of *New Internationalist* are not those with which they would ever want to be associated. Cornball males go for porno mags, car and fishing weeklies, sport annuals and boys' own comics, while their female counterparts feel safe from criticism behind the covers of womanies like *Woman's Realm* and *Woman's Own,* slimming mags and calorie counters. I imagine *Spare Rib* has no significance for most of them beyond a meal at the local Chinese restaurant. Cornballs don't generally read books at all, in case they encounter a new idea, but when they do they stick to Georgette Heyer, Harold Robbins, romantic and historical novels, thrillers, who-dun-its, westerns and creepies. They don't like anything 'heavy' and steer well clear of anything feminist or lefty, informative or progressive. Top notch cornballs stick firmly to *Tatler, Harpers & Queen, Country Life, Historic Houses, Who's Who, Debretts Peerage* and *Horse & Hound* — and they don't READ books, just collect them.

Cornballs from all walks of life share the view that lefties are loony and should be locked up or (preferably) shot. Feminism they see as a by-word for lesbianism and feminists as ugly, frustrated hags and spinsters who turn to feminism as a substitute for a husband. Cornballs rich and poor believe that the rich are rich because God ordained it and the poor are that way through their own stupidity, laziness and/or incompetence. All colours of cornball believe in the inherent superiority of the whites and both genders of cornball believe in the natural superiority of the male. Patriotism, the monarchy and the capitalist philosophy are all indispensable if you are of a cornball persuasion, as are such beliefs as Trades Unionism being bad for the country, fee-paying education being the inalienable right of those who can afford it and private enterprise being the only means of preserving the freedom of the individual. Vegetarianism is cranky or trendy, a woman's place is under him, blacks got rhythm and the unemployed could get a job if they weren't so lazy (or owned a bike). Left-wing plots are a constant obsession in every cornball brain-cell and Russian sympathisers hatch terrible and fiendish plans under every divan. Rape is the fault of women's libbers, nuclear war is inevitable without nuclear weapons and public transport would be vastly improved by cutting it in half.

Cornballs are invariably class conscious — either looking down or looking up, fighting to get in or struggling to stay out — although not many of them would admit it. "I'm as good as the next man", to a blue-collar cornball really means "I'm a bloody sight better than the wog next door", while "Some of my best friends live in council houses" is tacitly understood by other white-collar, owner-occupier cornballs to carry the message "But I wouldn't want them living next door". Cornballs' children are named according to the demands of their class and a working class Charles or Henry can find himself the object of a great deal of cornball derision from all sides if he is not prepared to concede to being a Charlie or a Harry; likewise, woebetide the reputation of upper echelon Ernest if he should ever allow himself to become an Ern. The wrong curtain material, an unfashionable shrub or an ill-considered combination of colours or textures can all be grist to the cornball mill of snobbery that labours under the label of 'good taste' — and earn the unfortunate guilty party a 'persona non grata' tag from which it will be virtually impossible to escape. No class is any less guilty than any other in its insistence upon sticking to the rules, although it is fairly obvious which end of the structure benefits most from it and it is noticeably more common for the bottom end to strive to emulate the top end than vice versa. Who, after all, who has been born into a class providing them with luxury is going to go out of their way to identify themselves with one that is dogged by poverty, unemployment, underprivilege and lack of opportunity when all they have to do to maintain their advantages for a lifetime is to stick to the rules of their class? This would seem to suggest that the lower end would be only too pleased to escape from the suffocating restrictions of the class system, but not so. The working class cornball, in fact, is just as adamant about avoiding 'pretentions' and just as hard on an errant peer who ignores the rules and stubbornly displays an antique heirloom in the front room of his council house as those who consider themselves his superiors would be, and he is therefore just as effective in keeping himself and his peers in their straitjacket of class limitation as are the other classes who are striving to keep him there.

These class divisions may make it seem, on the surface, as if working class cornball Pete has little in common with middle class cornball Oliver or upper class cornball Eustace but in fact their views are identical, it is only the way they choose to express them that differs. Pete's sexist outlook leads him into the boys' corner in the pub, where he makes a point of ignoring, insulting or belittling any woman who has the temerity to try to join in the conversation. He has little understanding of, and even less respect for, the gender that constitutes half the population of the world and has absolutely no idea how to communicate with it. Sexually, Pete is a dead loss, since his only real interest in it lies in proving his manhood for the sake of his arch critics in the boys' corner, so he gets it over with as quickly as possible. As with all cornballs, appearances are all important to Pete, so he talks a lot about sex in the form of innuendo and boasts a good deal about women and 'conquests', much of which usually owes more to his imagination than to his devastating charm in attracting women. The young Pete may make an effort to be sexually attractive for a time and worry about how he looks and smells, but this gradually wears off. After marriage less and less of his time will be spent at home with his wife and more and more of it with his cornball mates of pub and club. Effectively, cornball Pete is homo in every respect except sexual, since most of his waking hours are spent in the pursuit of impressing other men, and it is other men who satisfy the greater part of his emotional needs. He prefers men's company to women's, chooses men as his friends, confidantes and entertainers. Men provide him with his heroes and it is for other men he reserves all his greatest admiration: from other men's praise he derives his greatest satisfaction and only from the criticism of other men will he recognize any true indication of his own worth. Women are merely the bearers of his children, his bottle washers and meal providers, the occasional receptacles for the expression of his manhood and the receivers of his most scathing contempt. His disregard for her feelings manifests itself, in middle age or earlier, in a flabby beer gut, a stubbly growth, stinking breath and a truly remarkable display of sartorial inelegance. The act of copulation, after a night out with the boys, is interspersed with farts and belches and more often than not comes to a premature end with a trip to the bog to puke up the evening's indulgences. This thoroughly unattractive character can often be heard making remarks such as "Wouldn't touch HER with a barge pole" or "Just look at the state of *that*", or even more laughably "Cor, wouldn't mind a bit o' *that,* eh boy?". Yuk.

Oliver's sexist views and general contempt for women are no different to Pete's, but he expresses his prejudices in marginally different ways. His sexism in the office may be less pronounced and obvious than Pete's piece of flesh stuck on the factory wall, but is no less nauseating and damaging. Office Oliver spends his day in his personalized den, shuffling his 'important' papers around his leatherette desk and occasionally pouncing on his personal telephone to issue orders to his secretary in a clipped and peremptory tone that under any other circumstances would be called rude but which he excuses under the guise of efficiency. Occasionally he swings backwards and forwards on his buttonback, reclining chair and smiles smugly to himself as he surveys the general office outside with all the little hens clucking around and attending to his every need. With just a word he knows he can get a hundred photocopies done for him, telephone calls made on his behalf, lies told, letters typed and spelling mistakes and grammatical errors (HIS) corrected, stencils made, telexes sent, coffee and tea made just the way he likes it and a present for his wife chosen and bought. He sighs contentedly and pushes away his dirty cup and saucer for his little band of servants to wash up. It's just like being at home.

Upper class attitudes are hardly distinguishable from Oliver's, except that Henry and Eustace have more power and use it to good effect to ensure that women are kept in their subordinate position. Henry is in the Church to keep women out and male Gods in fashion, in the media to trivialise their achievements and to provide the working class with sexist jokes. Eustace ensures that places like the Stock Exchange, the City, Parliament and the Masons remain bastions of male power, while Julian takes charge of the law to ensure that women don't get too much alimony or cause men too much embarrassment. If Pete and Oliver are a pain in the arse, Henry and his ilk are devastating when it comes to making women's lives difficult.

The same general pattern applies to cornball racism. Pete ignores or insults blacks at work, joins the National Front and/or throws bricks, punches and lighted torches. Refined Oliver abhors such violence, interviews his quota of non-whites and employs all whites because "they were the best people for the job", regardless of minor considerations like better qualifications or mere lack of evidence one way or the other. Henry ensures that Gods are kept white, that blacks are subordinate in the Church, Parliament and any positions of power and that the immigration laws keep alive colonial attitudes and a belief in white superiority.

They all enjoy a good racist joke, all believe we are being 'swamped' by (black) aliens, all believe that white culture is the ONLY culture and none feels any guilt at all about white exploitation of the black world.

These, then, are the male cornballs — but what of the female of the ilk? Well, I've dealt with the males of the genre first because they and their attitudes are the PRIMARY cause of the state of the world at present and theirs is the PRIMARY source of power in whose clutches we writhe, but the corroboration they get from female cornballs is, nevertheless, an important factor in ensuring that the position stays as it is. As with the boys, there is a slight variation in cornball behaviour according to class distinctions, but basically the attitudes of cornball Shiel, Jean and Caroline are much the same. Cornball Shiel never really considers anything beyond marriage and children and, truth to tell, is probably even more boring than her slobby husband. She doesn't have any truck with 'women's lib' and thinks women can get their way with a bit of cunning (like a scheming and cajoling child whining after favours). This, despite her mother being totally and demonstrably dependent on the whims and moods of her slobby old man and despite the fact that many of her friends have ended up either poverty stricken as one parent families or terrorised by drunken, violent husbands. Cornball Shiel is adamant — Prince Charming may have taken a wrong turning but the rose-coloured dream world of Mills & Boon is surely just around the corner, complete with everlasting bliss.

Cornball Jean shares exactly the same views about 'women's libbers' and knows that being married, being feminine and having doors opened for you are all that life is really all about. She doesn't complain about her treatment at the hands of office Oliver and his ilk, and she won't hear a word of complaint from anyone else, either. She is quite happy in her subordinate role with her subordinate wage packet, she says. She doesn't believe in all this emancipation rubbish; God the father made women dependent and that's how they should stay. Jean fusses and clucks and tut-tuts with refined disapproval all day long about how men should open doors and carry her bags and how *awful* the women in the factory are and how *stupid* are the men with their silly strikes, how *terrible* it is the way standards and morals have been lowered since her mother was a girl and how she can't *abide* all those punks with their terrible hair and how she believes women should always look *smart* and *well turned out* and should *never* swear or fart . . . and so on, ad nauseam. All day she fusses about her nails and her hair and her dandruff and every day (as though obeying some unwritten office law) she dons a different smart, well-turned-out office outfit on which everybody is expected to comment. She knows little or nothing about anything that is going on in the world outside the confines of the office and cornball Close she inhabits and her comments on current issues are a mixture of hand-me-downs from reactionary parents and hubby and the regurgitated garbage churned out by the *Mail* and *Express*.

Cornball Jean is very conscious of office status and will inform you, right from the word go, who is whose boss, who is more important than who else, whose boots should be licked the cleanest and who should be kept in their place as a subordinate. Office etiquette and procedure constitute a large part of her preoccupations in life and she will very swiftly let you know if your behaviour is in any way out of line.

"Mr. Pratt likes his typing done IMMEDIATELY, dear, so leave office Joe's and do HIS as soon as it arrives. He's a very important man, so don't forget to grovel. Mr. Pillock doesn't like it if you don't knock on his door. He likes you to knock three times, but not too loudly and then call 'Mr. Pillock, may I come in please'? He doesn't like it if you don't wear tights in the summer, however hot it is, and he prefers you to wear make-up. They don't like trousers on women here (and neither do I, actually), and they prefer it if you don't wear flat shoes. And between you and me, dear, I WOULD do something about my hair, if I were you. Mr. Wanka hates you to put calls directly through to him, so always put them through to me first, then I'll go in to his office and ask him if he wants to take the call (he doesn't like the switchboard to do it) and then if he does I put it through on his phone. He has two and an eighth sugars in his tea from the little silver spoon and two and a half in his coffee, with half a Sweetex. He hates chocolate biscuits, so make sure he gets those coconut ones with the little red sweet on top. Make sure he doesn't get broken ones and brush any crumbs off for him. . ."

Cornball Olivers rely heavily on such subservience to keep the hierarchy intact, which makes the Jeans of this world willing participants in their own subjugation, a point which the Olivers of this world will be quick to point out if the ugly question of equality ever raises its head.

Cornball Caroline fulfils much the same functions and abides by much the same code of behaviour and whereas her wealth and background may cushion her against much of the exploitation and humiliation experienced by Jean, it does not afford her any more respect from her male counterparts, any greater (relative) status or any more opportunities to make full use of her individual capabilities. Sooner or later her spirit will be crushed and subjugated just as effectively as are Shiel's and Jean's under the weight of male dominance — and just as inevitably, she will have helped to do it.

This, then, concludes an outline of the cornball mentality, on an individual basis, which leads me to the question of 'national identity', and a further examination of what makes the cornball tick.

2. CORNBALL TRADITIONALISTS

I've heard it said that this country no longer has a National Identity and that the British culture has become so fragmented amongst different races, religions and classes that it is no longer recognisable as a definable entity but unfortunately this is far from true. The dominant "British" culture (defined by a powerful minority, upheld by established institutions and supported by the cornballs) is still alive in all its Victorian inflexibility, and steeped in every kind of imaginable prejudice. The dominant British culture is white, patriarchal, authoritarian — and nauseatingly pompous. The "British" attitude to non-whites is patronising and insulting and is the product of years of empire-building exploitation of black races throughout the world; the

"British" attitude to women is patronising and insulting and is the product of years of exploitation built on male arrogance and presumption. There may be slight variations according to class, but overall the British "National Identity" is characterised by its common thread of sexism, racism, snobbery and arrogance. Why, then, are the cornballs so keen to keep alive this truly undesirable culture, and what is it about these thoroughly unpleasant characteristics that they feel so proud to possess and insist are so indispensable? You may well ask, but I think it is all connected with habit and bound to the sacred and inviolable area of 'tradition'.

The one thing that stands out above all else about the cornballs is their hatred of change together with their conviction that 'what has always been always will be' and, moreover BECAUSE it has always been it must be right and should not be challenged. For this reason, habit forms a large part of their character and however nasty, undesirable and damaging the habit may be, cornballs will still be loth to change it. They are addicted to convention the same way that the inveterate smoker is addicted to tobacco, not because it does them any good — on the contrary, more often than not it does them considerable *harm* — but because they have done it for so long it has become part of their identity. Much as smokers fear that if they give up the habit they will no longer identify, or be identified, with their smoker friends whose 'smoking' character revolves around 'living dangerously' and making jokes about health freaks, so cornballs fear that if they get caught reading *'Spare Rib'* or start objecting to racist or sexist behaviour they may be jeered at by the boys in the cafe or the wags at the office, or branded as a 'women's libber'. The habit of believing they are always right and should not have to justify their beliefs makes it virtually impossible to conduct an interesting conversation with cornballs because within moments of them sniffing a controversial subject their eyes start darting around the room in nervous apprehension and they start to fidget, cough, scratch, look out of the window and generally convey an impression of total lack of interest. Eventually they will either kill the conversation with a racist/sexist joke or, if they know you well, lament the fact that you have no sense of humour and exhort you not to take life so seriously. Cornballs view outsiders as a dangerous and unacceptable threat to their security and while there's nothing they like better than to get together with other cornballs to exchange well worn platitudes and jokes about coons, women's libbers, brown ricers and poofters, there's nothing they like less than having the cosy little scene upset by outside (i.e. different) opinions.

Cornball custom, habit and tradition form the very essence of British culture and it is difficult to determine where one ends and the other begins. Where, for example, would you place fish and chips, Christmas pudding, London taxis, roast beef, door to door milk delivery, royal ceremonies? Custom? Habit? Tradition? Are they dispensable habits like LSD (the currency kind!) and the diminishing English breakfast, or indispensable traditions? What is so indispensable about traditions, especially if they are *bad* traditions? What is it that makes cornballs go all dewy-eyed at the mention of 'British Tradition' and so vehemently defensive at any mention that it may be threatened? Can it really be Christmas pudding they are all so concerned about? No, I can't believe it. Somehow, the magic key to unlock unabashed floods of cornball sentimentality lies with words like 'Heritage,' 'Legacy', 'Birthright', 'Monarchy' and 'Land of Hope and Glory'. But *WHY?* What has any of those things to do with the average British citizen who merely inherits poverty, inequality and underprivilege? The Royals, by comparison — together with the established upper class — inherit vast tracts of land, estates for their brats' wedding presents, paintings by old masters, exquisitely carved furniture, most of the wealth of the country and the power to make sure it is all kept in the family. I can certainly see why the rich would go dewy-eyed over tradition and I can see why they would not wish to see the Monarchy disappear, why 'Land of Hope and Glory' would have a particular eye-wetting significance for THEM — but what is there about all that for the average citizen to be so defensive about? Eat your heart out, Robert Tressell, The Ragged Trousered cornballs are still thriving. But then, I am missing the point about the real fascination with Royalty, aren't I? By carping about greed and inequality and such like I am merely being a killjoy. For who but a killjoy could fail to see the connection of the Royals with fairy tale palaces in which everybody is pure white and beautiful, where love and honour and all the BRITISH things abound and where people live happily ever after in marital bliss in breathtakingly beautiful surroundings of flowers, flowing streams and vast expanses of estate? Who am I to be unmoved by the vision of clean-shaven, youthful princes marrying be-jewelled princesses in long white robes and being transported to sumptuous palaces in glass carriages pulled by teams of pure white horses? Shame on me, for sure, for selfishly wishing to smash illusions and expose the charade for the ridiculous, romantic dream it is, fostered by the rich and kindled by *The Sun* to give the dispossessed a vision of hope. Sad but true, the unpalatable reality of married life for an overwhelming majority of people is that it is fraught with problems of all descriptions, marred by financial worries and dogged by the restrictions of rigid role-playing. Demonstrably, the vast majority of women are NOT content living in the unnatural and suffocating position of isolation and intellectual starvation presented by the patriarchal nuclear family and men, demonstrably, do NOT in most cases react to women's dependence with everlasting love and an overwhelming desire to protect them against the harsh outside world. The evidence of the farcical nature of the fantasy can be witnessed every day in the divorce courts and in the alarming and ever increasing figures for rape, wife beating, baby battering and child molestation within the family quite apart from the staggering numbers of women taking some kind of pill or alcohol to escape the reality of the fairy tale dream, yet the myth persists and the Royals live out their lives in royal palaces like characters in a Christmas pantomime to keep alive the patriarchal fantasy. To me, there is something highly immoral and slightly sick about using other people as surrogates for failed hopes and broken dreams, and something strangely sad and pathetic about the players who are engaged in the deception.

While the female cornball clings to the romance of handsome princes and glittering princesses, her male counterpart clings tenaciously to the Monarchy as proof of his own dubious worth. Much as the football fan will feed vicariously on the success of his team, desperately hoping that some of that success will rub off on him, so the Royalist clings to the Royal Family as seeming evidence of the possibilities offered by being 'British'. He laments the wealth, the power and the respect that are, in reality, lacking in his own life, so he dreams of Empire, waves his flag and bows in homage to the Royals. He buys his coronation mug, displays his picture of Di and Charles and glows with pride at the greatness of Great Britain, the power of the Empire, the superiority of the British. If he can't command respect for himself in his everyday existence then by God he'll do it through the Empire. The fact that the Empire no longer exists and the Royal Family are merely a band of parasites living in luxury at everybody else's expense is something he, the eternal royalist cornball is not prepared even to think about. The fact that however much Empire there is or was *HE* will still remain the powerless, over-worked and underpaid little squirt he has always been and that any amount of flag-waving and God-save-the-Queening will not give him or his offspring the respect he craves, cannot weaken his manic and obsequious worship of the rich.

Old habits die hard and the habit of nostalgically worshipping the long expired power of the British nation to manipulate the rest of the world is dying harder than most. But die it must, however painfully, if we are not to become the laughing stock of the world. The Royals, enacting their ridiculous and anachronistic walkabouts amongst 'ordinary people' and 'colourful barbarians', are fast becoming figures of derision for the more progressive peoples of the world and an embarrassment to the people of this country. If the rest of us are to be allowed to hold our heads up and stop cringing in embarrassment, the Great British cornball has got to admit, once and for all, that the Empire is dead. The days when Britain ruled the waves and called the tune are *OVER*, and instead of viewing the Empire as a loss to be lamented he must learn to view it as a burden of guilt from which we can at last be freed, with a little effort. The cultural legacy etched by the cruelty, inhumanity, exploitation and arrogance of our ancestors is not something for any of us to rejoice in, it is something to feel thoroughly ashamed of. I cannot hold up my head and say I am proud to be British all the while the shadow of past atrocities is hanging over me, and the cloud will not be lifted until the Great British cornball learns a little humility; learns to see himself as the pompous, conceited and totally ridiculous figure he presents to the rest of humanity. If the Great British cornball wishes to sing national anthems with pride and credibility he has to to have a drastic re-think about his national identity, because as it stands at the moment he's got precious little to sing about. He has got to cast off his arrogant assumption that the world is there to do his bidding and put in a bit of real hard work to achieve a culture based on compassion rather than on cruelty and exploitation. If he wants admiration he has got to make a genuine effort to understand the people he has spent so long despising and to try to atone for the wrongs of the past. He must recognise that many of his sacred traditions are steeped in blood, rooted in barbarity and ignorance and no more acceptable in the 20th century than is the outrageous behaviour of the white South Africans.

And at the same time as the male cornball is learning long overdue humility, the female of the genre could do well to learn a bit of realism and commonsense. Handsome princes, glass carriages, happy-ever-after endings?? How can she ever expect to command any respect when she refuses to grow up and leave behind the child's world of fairy tales and fantasy? Or does she, I wonder, want to spend her whole life being treated like a little girl in a frilly pink party dress being bounced on daddy's knee? Sometimes I think they both get exactly what they deserve — the trouble is, they drag all the rest of us down with them.

3. CORNBALL MYTHOLOGY

Cornballs are recognizable not just by their rigid adherence to the dictates of convention and tradition but also by their addiction to a series of myths about the human condition, coupled with a serious inability to appreciate the anomalous relationship between their own convictions and the conflicting evidence presented by the overall human experience. The first of these, the moral majority myth, relies upon a disturbingly distorted self-image and an unreasoning self-righteousness on the part of the cornballs to keep it alive.

Both middle England and middle America revolve around the same cornball visions of morality and are steeped in exactly the same kind of self-righteous hypocrisy. Cornball morality on both sides of the Atlantic has little or nothing to do with how human beings treat one another or with how much suffering is caused by their individual or collective actions, but EVERYthing to do with who sleeps with who, how often, what gender they are and whether they go to Church on Sundays. Never mind if they exploit other people for their own selfish ends; never mind if they knowingly inflict drought and starvation on thousands of people by cutting down trees to make a profit; never mind if they harass, persecute and demean anybody not of the 'right' colour, creed or gender; never mind if they put people out of work in their hundreds of thousands and leave them to exist on the poverty line; never mind if they support and engineer foreign policies that cause torture, atrocity and death; never mind if they sell arms to leaders of cruel and exploitative regimes; never mind about all that. Just as long as they don't commit such unpardonable sins as falling in love with a member of their own sex or sleeping with their neighbour's wife they will still be regarded as honourable, respectable, *MORAL* citizens beyond reproach. This façade of moral respectability in the face of obvious moral bankruptcy in every other direction is not easy for the cornballs to maintain, and nobody knows better than they do the constant threat posed to their image of moral superiority by their own individual desires. The self-created pedestal would, therefore, be extremely fragile without some external evidence of their own moral worth, some socially constructed criterion against which to measure their level of goodness. Hence the myth of the criminal as moral inferior to which the cornball tenaciously clings.

Vast numbers of people in our unequal society are made to feel angry and resentful all through their lives. As children they are often humiliated, sometimes beaten and constantly have their feelings and opinions crushed underfoot by insensitive adults in the name of 'character building' and 'fitting in to a competitive world'. Throughout their adult lives they are taunted by unobtainable goals, goaded by callous employers, tricked into feeling inferior by an inflexible and pre-determined hierarchy, constantly forced to measure their own 'failure' against the 'success' of others, bored rigid by repetitive and meaningless occupations, thrown out of work, harassed by money worries, humiliated and degraded by inequality. Some people react to this constant assault on their self-esteem with violence or attempt to escape from their financial nightmares by 'unlawful' means, and these people are branded **CRIMINALS**. Those who are not termed 'criminal' are thus able to imagine that this makes them somehow superior, which is the real reason behind the malicious obsession with punishment exhibited by the cornballs and not, as is commonly supposed, that they believe in its effectiveness as a deterrent. Even the cornball knows, given the amount of evidence in its favour, that the worse people are treated by society the greater is the possibility that they will commit crimes, despite threats of punishment — and that if nobody tries to help them change the circumstances from which they were trying to escape on the outside they will return to prison time and again, regardless of how badly they are treated there. Even the cornballs must be aware that violence breeds violence and that brutilizing people merely makes them more resentful, more violent and more likely to want to seek retribution from what they see as an uncaring society. Even cornballs must have noticed that small boys continue to misbehave despite the threat of a whack on the arse and even cornballs must know that our prisons are overflowing with people who had not heard they were supposed to be a deterrent. It is therefore not feasible to suppose that the cornballs actually BELIEVE in the effectiveness of punishment as a deterrent against crime, so their outbursts in favour of harsher and harsher sentences are only understandable in terms of their own fears, their own feelings of inadequacy and their own shortcomings. Their moral outrage and the snarling insults they heap upon the criminal are a manifestation of the same pain, anger, frustration and bitterness that lead criminals along their destructive paths, and the same fury that makes cornballs spit venomous hatred at blacks, gays, women, Jews and vegetarians can be heard in hysterical shrieks against the criminal. A little excavation of the cornball psyche soon reveals that *"Kill him, beat him, hang him, tear him to shreds, castrate him, lock him away for a hundred years, make him suffer, make him pay, crucify him . . ."* translated means *"Let* HIM *atone for all the pain that has been inflicted on* ME *and let* HIM *suffer so that I may feel morally superior"* and is a sad but dangerous indication of the lack of security the cornballs suffer in their attempts to justify their frail and empty definition of 'morality'.[1]

The final, and most prevalent, of the major cornball myths is their most sacred cow, for without it they would be hard put to find a suitable excuse for their outrageous selfishness. I'm sure than anybody who has ever indulged in one of those displays of conditioned responses that labours under the misnomer of a 'discussion' with a cornball will undoubtedly have encountered the standard cornball escape route from any tight corner — namely the ubiquitous, shoulder-shrugging, "It's human nature". This ends all further argument and infers that any attempt to alter whatever it was you were proposing to alter is unrealistic, idealistic, utterly pointless and not worth further consideration. It signifies, in effect, that the cornball, having run out of standard responses, platitudes and quotes from *The Sun*, and unable to deter the adversary with sexist quips and personal insults, wants to escape with the minimum loss of pride. It is futile to pursue the point about human nature because by this time the cornball is yawning, fidgeting and eyeing the door, and any mention of the role of social conditioning in influencing human behaviour will be met with varying degrees of irritation. The cornball is adamant; human beings are aggressive, competitive and chained to roles and behaviour patterns by biology. They are incapable of altering their circumstances because their actions are dictated by instinct. They are unable to look at themselves and alter their behaviour, even if it is in their own interests

1. *This same moral insecurity is the basis of the hysterical cornball opinion of the USSR as "sin bin of Godless depravity and moral inferiority" that is constantly, and irresponsibly, fanned by those in power in the West.*

and those of the survival of the planet, because they are too stupid. Even though aggression and competition demonstrably leads to dangerous world friction, to waste, to starvation and to human misery on a grand scale, human beings can do nothing to change this to enable the world to revolve around co-operation because human beings have no control over their destiny. Nothing can be done to improve the way the world conducts its affairs so that people do not have to starve and live in grinding poverty because human beings are too selfish and greedy; and nothing can be done to alter individual circumstances because human beings are too lazy, apathetic, addicted to convention and snobbery and pre-occupied with appearances. Human beings are perfectly happy in subordinate, subservient positions and enjoy being starved, beaten, insulted and dictated to, and even if they don't, nothing can be done about it because . . . it is human nature.

There ARE human beings on the earth who fit the description above, without a doubt. They are greedy, competitive, mean-spirited and narrow-minded. They give a damn for nothing or nobody except themselves, are incapable of seeing themselves and the world from any other point of view but their own and are totally unprepared to do anything at all to change anything at all. They are the same people who, in recent years, have reacted with venomous disapproval against The Women's Movement, The Animal Rights Movement, The Peace Movement, The Civil Rights Movement, The Gay Rights Movement and the food revolution. They are a shrill, highly irresponsible minority that the vast majority of the population would be pleased to see the back of, but they represent an indispensable vehicle for establishment propaganda and are therefore never short of support from self-interested bodies of power speaking through the media and acting through established institutions. This gives an illusion of substance both to their numbers and to their morality and with a characteristic disregard for truth they have elected to call themselves the *moral majority*. I call them cornballs.

RICH

HITE
ORLD

MALE

WHITE SOUTH AFRICA

★ Militarised Power Structure instills fear and subservience into blacks

★ Church, law, media and government uphold the status quo and enforce established white, cultural values

★ Colonial whites use land of indigenous population for their own use and largely to their own advantage

★ Large corporations with massive capital use cheap, black labour to extract resources and make huge profits in manufactured goods

★ Whites indoctrinate blacks into feeling inferior by limiting their opportunities for self-expression, keeping them impoverished, badly informed and dependent, belittling their achievements, mocking their traditions and divorcing them from any sense of their own historical culture and identity. By the same tactics they are prevented from realizing the extent of the injustice and exploitation they have suffered

★ Whites have comfortable, well-paid administrative and professional occupations and live in sumptuous surroundings with black, domestic servants

★ FIRST-CLASS   CITIZENS.

BLACK SOUTH AFRICA
POOR

There is a small point at which the opposing forces overlap. It is called TOKENISM

★ Powerless — intimidated and dominated by whites

★ Live according to white, cultural values

★ No autonomy. No economic independence

★ Poorly paid in menial, boring, dirty and/or dangerous occupations

★ Most of their lives served in the interests of white profits and white comfort (i.e. so that whites can have televisions, Martinis, tea, coffee, hard-wood doors, private cars, imported food, large houses, holiday homes, swimming pools, domestic servants, private boats, marble baths, hi-fi equipment, electric guitars, gourmet dinners, jet travel, washing machines, electric mixers . . .)

The only significant difference between the oppression of South African blacks by South African whites and the oppression of third world blacks by rich world whites is DISTANCE: we may not SEE the effects of multi-national exploitation and we may not experience, close at hand, the effects of our Governments' foreign policies to steal third world resources, to use their populations as cheap labour and to arm and support their oppressors — but those factors are just as evil as anything that is happening in South Africa, and we are just as guilty.

★ SECOND-CLASS CITIZENS

LACK
ORLD

FEMALE

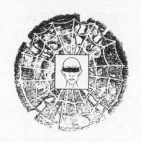

SECTION TWO

UPHOLDING THE STATUS QUO

At various stages throughout our history the human race has been presented with challenges of social and environmental disruption which have necessitated a decision to alter our behaviour patterns or face varying degrees of discomfort. Every time this has occurred there has been an element amongst the population that has clung fearfully to the status quo, stubbornly and short-sightedly maintaining that 'what is now has always been and must always remain so'.

At no time in our history has this cornball attitude been so cruelly devastating to such a huge percentage of the world's inhabitants, so morally unjustifiable or so potentially disastrous. The following pages are an attempt to document what 'The Status Quo' that cornballs are so determined to uphold signifies for vast numbers of people throughout the world, the amount of suffering it is causing to both human beings and to animals and the dangers it is presenting to the whole future of the planet itself.

1. RICH WORLD POOR WORLD

☆ *At least 450 million of the world's inhabitants suffer from malnutrition and hunger.*

☆ *The developing world has 70% of the world's people but only 10% of the world's wealth.*

☆ *Ten to twenty-five million people die every year from diseases caused by dirty or inadequate supplies of water and poor sanitation.*

☆ *The chances of a child dying in the first year can be up to ten times higher in developing countries.*

These fundamental realities, and the appalling suffering that they signify, are as water off a duck's back to cornballs who believe that blacks are lazy, feckless and totally responsible for their own miserable fate. 'If they didn't breed so fast and were to get off their black arses and to do a real day's work all their problems could be solved'. In any event, say the cornballs, it's nothing to do with us; it's not our problem.

Four hundred years ago there was little difference in the living standards of Northern Europe from Asia, Africa or the Americas. There were obviously large cultural variations, but each land, or region of it, had its own resources, its own beauty and its own means of survival and independence. In terms of natural resources, many third world countries were, and still are, way ahead of many of today's rich countries (Britain is a prime example). So how did the third world, now named, get tricked into the position of poverty and dependence that they are in today? Primarily, through colonialism. Innovations in ship-building and weapons design enabled the countries of Northern Europe (most notably Spain and Portugal, Britain and France, but not forgetting the Dutch) to reach across oceans to dominate other peoples and plunder their lands. Latin America provided great wealth for Europe when she was robbed of her minerals, and enabled merchants from Europe to go on further plundering forays overseas. Long distance trade voyages were highly lucrative and axes, muskets and blankets were taken to West Africa to be exchanged for slaves, who were used to work the sugar and tobacco plantations in the Americas, and later those producing tea, coffee, jute and rubber throughout Asia and Africa. These goods would then be shipped back to Europe to make fat profits for the Europeans, who had stolen the land and resources and paid nothing for the labour — a real Tory dream. These voyages had the effect of stimulating new manufacturing industries in Europe to supply the goods for trade, and iron and textile industries abounded. North America, rich in prairie land for farming, in oil and in minerals, was torn from the unsuspecting and often overtrusting native population by means of cheap liquor and guns and this last act finally set the scene for today's poor world. As the colonists developed their own industries back home the colonies were left undeveloped save for the plantations that served Europe with raw materials.

This pattern of producing raw materials for other countries is one that still continues for the third world and is one that is very difficult for them to break, by dint of the continuing greed and selfishness of the colonial bosses of old. Around sixty per cent of the foreign exchange of the developing world comes from one or two primary commodities, examples being cotton from Chad, copper from Zambia, sugar from Cuba, bananas from Honduras — the pattern is similar throughout the third world. These 'cash' crops, and many others, have little or no nutritional value. They were not designed to feed the people who live on the land but to satisfy the whims of those in distant lands, and to make fat profits for the few at the expense of the many. Around fourteen developing countries rely for their livelihood on coffee and a vast acreage of land — often prime agricultural land — is used to grow this nutritionally worthless crop when it could — and should — be used to feed the undernourished local population. Instead, much of the money earned from these cash crops has to be used to pay for imported food, which is very expensive and usually goes to the rich minority and not to the people who are in dire need of it.

Why, then, do they not escape from this situation by growing cereals and beans to feed themselves? Well partly, it has to be said, because the rich minority of many of these countries are quite happy to continue getting rich on foreign exchange to buy themselves beef steaks and luxury consumer items and to hell with the starving majority, but for those who would like to make the break many obstacles have to be overcome. For a start, such a change necessitates capital for agricultural equipment and research, and to recondition the soil to accommodate the new crop. It also necessitates capital on which to survive whilst the changeover is made. Most third world countries not only do not have any capital, they are deeply in debt to the rich world and have to pay back aid, so they have to have a cash crop of some description. Why not grow more of the existing cash crops to gain capital? Because the very nature of these crops makes the price they attract unstable and demand fluctuating. They are not necessities, so if times get hard in rich countries the first things that get cut down or taken off the shopping list are things like coffee, cocoa, tea and all non-essentials — the very things the poor world are dependent upon for their survival. The recent health purge against sugar has cut down considerably the demand for it in many rich countries.

Why, then, can't they put up their prices to compensate for the lessening demand? Because the RICH countries are the ones who control prices and they organize things to suit themselves. Import tariffs on manufactured goods from third world countries are considerably higher than on their raw materials, which makes it prohibitive for poor countries to enter the competition in this field on a grand scale and enables the rich world countries to continue to get cheap raw materials which they process and market themselves to make vast profits.

Keeping things as they are throughout the world means keeping the 'right' people in control of poor countries (they may be sons-of-bitches but they're OUR sons-of-bitches). If the general population of the country revolts against virtual slave labour and starvation and instates a socialist government bent on such ideals as making the country independent, feeding, clothing and giving the people a decent standard of living and educating the masses about what is *REALLY* going on in the world, then rich investors from the rich world are going to suffer, since the first ones to get kicked out will be the exploitative, rich-world multi-nationals that are bleeding the country of its resources and using its people as cheap labour. Chile tried such an adventure under Allende. So has Bolivia. So has Nicaragua. So has Jamaica. So has Grenada. So have numerous other third world countries throughout the world. And what happens, with sickening regularity? USA 'military advisors' appear on the scene. 'Communist threat' propaganda is circulated around the West. 'Reds in our own backyard' hysteria sweeps the great US of A. And before you can say 'Viva Nicaragua' a brand new, ultra right-wing, exploitative dictator is back in control to terrorise the people and subjugate their will. The freedom fighters (guerrillas/terrorists) are liquidated in their thousands, oppression, misery, poverty and starvation are restored to the majority, fabulous wealth to a small minority, peace of mind to rich world shareholders and vast profits to the multi-nationals. Such is the power of life and death that the rich world holds over the poor.

The poor of the world are kept poor by quite deliberate economic policies — not by accident, laziness, ineptitude, inferiority or rampant reproduction. Third world countries are not free entities who have made a poor job of organising their affairs, and the colonial bosses have not relinquished their hold over them. Twentieth century conquistadores, in the guise of multi-national trading conglomerates, are still calling the tune, plundering distant lands of their resources and using the labour of native populations to line their own pockets. Under the yoke of their domination millions of people are starved, beaten, tortured, worked to death and deprived of everything that allows human beings a vestige of dignity. Nothing much has changed since those days of yore when the conquering heroes first set foot in distant lands to violate the rights of their inhabitants in the name of civilization, masking the skull and crossbones with a flag of Christianity.

Is this justifiable? Is this humane? Is this supportable? Is this MORAL? The cornballs believe it is.

2. RICH FOLK POOR FOLK

It has been estimated that the top one per cent of people in Britain own 80% of privately held stocks and shares.

In 1973 (it won't have changed much with Thatcher's regime) less than half of one per cent of the population owned nearly 60% of all the land in England and Wales.

It is estimated that the aristocracy own 18 million acres of land and 200 titled families, even after death duties, have still managed to retain estates of 5,000 acres of more — often considerably more.

In 1976-7 the top bracket stockbrokers, jobbers and insurers in the City each earned an average of £65,000 a year, the top solicitors earned £56,000 and accountants £52,000. Directors may receive hundreds of pounds for half a day's work. City administrators and professional people gain further huge profits from personal knowledge regarding the buying and selling of land and shares.

High rates of income tax have had little effect on the rich because they have expert knowledge regarding the loopholes they can skip through. The distribution of wealth in Britain has changed little in the last 30 years, except that the rich have got slightly richer with the advent of Thatcherism.

"Hard work seldom makes anyone rich. The secret to wealth is to have others work hard for you".

Michael Parenti, American social scientist,
from New Internationalist, July 1984

I confess to being dumbfounded as to why cornballs who have absolutely nothing by comparison are so defensive of a system that allows others the opportunity to accumulate so very much. Why, I continually ask, are you not ANGRY that while you are struggling to pay your gas bill, others are spending thousands of pounds, sometimes millions, on an item of furniture, an antique, a picture or a postage stamp? Why do you not question the morality of a system that enables some people to **INHERIT** more than you can ever hope to earn in a lifetime? Why does your sense of justice and fair play not scream in protest against those who can spend upwards of £3,000 in school fees each year for each of their children while you can barely feed and clothe your own? Why are you not incensed at the knowledge that some people, for no other reason than having been born into the right family, can send their children to dancing classes, swimming classes, music classes and riding schools, buy them the BEST sports equipment, give them the very BEST protection against the elements, the most NUTRITIOUS food, the most EXPENSIVE medical attention, give them everything their little hearts could desire in toys, books, ponies, watches, bicycles, calculators, stereo equipment, rifles, riding gear, cars, ski-ing holidays, educational trips abroad . . . provide them with EVERY chance the little darlings could possible have to get the BEST start in life . . . while YOU have to leave your kids at the mercy of cuts in education which may leave them without proper books and school equipment and not even a hot meal at lunchtime? Why do you not rebel in anger and disgust against those who have a private estate in the country, a luxury flat in London, a villa in Gibraltar and an account in a Swiss bank — and who call those living on £60 a week from Social Security "Scroungers"? Where, I ask them, is your pride? Where is the commonsense you were born with that should tell you how ludicrous and insupportable it all is? But I never get an answer, beyond the fact that it is human nature and that I should not be so 'envious'.

It is a strange and unaccountable thing, but cornballs at the bottom end of the social scale actually imagine that their philanthropic attitudes to the rich and powerful somehow make them respected, but they are quite wrong. On the contrary, the 'plebs' are the butt of the greater part of upper-crust humour, the salt-of-the-earth worker the most despised and lampooned of all God's creatures. For who can respect those who are so willing, uncomplainingly, to lay down their lives in the interests of somebody else's luxurious life-style whilst they themselves can barely keep their own and their families' body and soul together? How could the rich do anything but despise anybody so easily duped? The rich are not grateful to the poor fools who spend their lives working in soul-destroying, dangerous and unhealthy jobs in their interests, they merely search for better ways of getting more out of them for less return —

and replace them as often as possible by machines that do not demand even the most pitiful of wages. Politicians — especially Tories — do not talk in terms of workers' lives, or needs, or happiness, or welfare, they talk in terms of industry, output, over-manning and profit. They say "We must knuckle down and become more competitive ... tighten our belts, cut down on public expenditure and put the economy back on its feet", but they don't mean 'WE' at all, since they do not include themselves or the rest of their class in their programme of 'necessary' austerity: they mean YOU the scab, YOU the union basher, YOU the social security informer, YOU the worker, YOU the poor, YOU the low income/unemployed cornball. THEY will not be put out of work by the simple expedient of being 'more competitive'. THEY will still have their expensive health insurance so THEY will not be affected by cuts in the health service and THEIR children will not be affected by cuts in education because THEIR children will be at expensive private schools. THEY will still be living in *EXACTLY* the style to which they are accustomed, it is *YOU* and *ME* who will suffer. They couldn't care less about you and your kids and your aged parents, your health, your children's health and education, whether you have money for food or to go on holiday or money to pay the gas bill to keep yourself warm in the winter and eat hot food — THEY are only interested in their profits and their investments, in maintaining their standard of living, sending their kids on expensive holidays, making sure THEY can still eat roast duck and caviar, go to the theatre, go to the opera, go to 'charity' balls, throw parties for their daughters' 21st birthdays, buy their sons sports cars and cabin cruisers — YOU and your miserable family are just the means to this end and if you have to be unemployed, cold, poverty-stricken and desperate, *That is the price you must pay to maintain their privileged and excessive life style.*

On a recent TV programme an economist who was interviewed by some unemployed youngsters asked them with thinly disguised contempt in a 'cultured' accent "What *right* have you got to EXPECT a living? Why SHOULDN'T you work 40 hours a week for £25? Why SHOULD you expect to do work you enjoy; you should be prepared to do whatever is available — at whatever money is offered to you. You know, there *IS* no unemployment in this country — there's PLENTY of low paid work but nobody is prepared to do it, they all want more money. £50 per week is a jolly good wage". This sums up the contempt these bastards have for the menials who uphold their standard of living and I can only ask the cornballs out there in some exasperation 'what is so attractive about such a status quo? Why do you waste so much time and energy carping about "scroungers" on the S.S. when the *REAL* scroungers are robbing you and your children blind? Why are you not ashamed to allow a handful of upper class twits to lead you by the nose and treat you and your family with such contempt?'

Any answers on a postcard to *'The Sun'* who will no doubt be delighted to print them.

3. A WOMAN'S PLACE

Girls and boys go out to play and learn your lessons well
Girls on the left and boys on the right
Take your positions, prepare for the fight.

Boys to the fore and girls are a bore
No points for loving, ten points for gore.
Compete with your neighbour and make sure you WIN
Weakness is cissy and losing's a sin.

Wop the Argies, sink the Hun
Nuke the Commies . . . it's all such good FUN.

Girls and boys go out to play and learn your lessons well
But don't come to us with hearts full of pain
when the dreams are all broken, your children are slain.
No don't come to us and wail and sob because
we were just guardians, doing our job.

An important part of maintaining the status quo is keeping women in the home so that they can be drawn upon as cheap and unpaid labour while providing a captive market for the consumer rubbish churned out to keep the capitalist[1] system alive. Of course it is infinitely debatable what was the original motive behind the subjugation of women within the framework of economics;

a) whether the birth of patriarchal economic structures was a manifestation of an already existing male desire to control women, either through fear, or envy of women's creative capacity, or the desire to be assured of guaranteed sexual gratification

or

b) whether women's biology merely made them easily identifiable targets to be used in divide-and-rule tactics (like different skin colour, accent, religious sect, etc. etc.) to uphold a system in which some men could attain power over other men as a defence against male violence (or competition) — with wordly wealth a mere symbolic by-product

or

c) whether women were sacrificial lambs at the altar of good old fashioned greed, with accumulation of wealth uppermost on the list of priorities

or

d) whether it was a combination of all three . . .

but whichever it was, the results have spelled disaster for both sexes all around the world.

The evident fact that men in general, and cornball men in particular, don't have the first idea what women are all about isn't too surprising, since the patriarchal establishment, together with cornball parents, do everything possible to ensure that this state of affairs forms a dominant part of our society. Right from the word go, when little girls are dressed in pink and little boys in blue (in case, horror of horrors, somebody should make a mistake), the progress and development of the sexes is made distinctive and divisive. Cornball parents can be heard every day inflicting their damaging messages on

1. *I say 'capitalist' because that happens to be the particular economic system under which I live, but that is not to lose sight of the fact that women's emancipation is not an automatic corollary of ALL forms of socialism. Patriarchal socialism speaks for itself — and ANY social system that is constructed around wealth-creating economics and which (necessarily) divides society into productive — reproductive, paid — unpaid will make a large majority of women the subordinate (and dependent) sex.*

unsuspecting little minds, taking advantage of innocent little bodies who trustingly believe that Mummy and Daddy know best and who little imagine how Mummy and Daddy are fucking up their little lives as they mindlessly drone out the platitudes passed down through the cornball generations, from boring grandparent to brainwashed parent to unwary child.

'Boys will be boys' (i.e. boys should be permitted, if not encouraged, to be overbearing, selfish, spiteful, greedy and egocentric).

'Little boys don't cry, William. Don't act like a silly girl'.

'Boys shouldn't be expected to wash up, Jean. Don't make a fool of the child in front of his friends. Tell Cathy to do it'.

'Don't namby pamby him woman. Do you want him to turn into a bloody queer?' . . . and so on. Of course, the cornball will tell you there's nothing WRONG with all this, that it's all quite harmless. Cornballs are not noted for their perspicacity, so it is usually fruitless trying to explain to them that what you do and say to LITTLE people will later have an effect on how they act when they become BIG people, and that if you divide the sexes and teach them to dislike one another as children they will find it difficult to love and understand one another when they become adults. If little boys don't respect little girls, then men will not respect women. If little boys are taught to play with guns (or if you are one of those who believe in the inherent evil of all men, ALLOWED to play with guns), then the chances are that much greater that MEN will want to play with items of destruction. If little girls are taught to be helpless and incapable, women will be helpless and incapable. If little boys are encouraged to be self-centred, men will be self-centred. If boys are taught that it is natural and advisable for them to be hard hearted and insensitive, MEN will be hard hearted and insensitive to the plight of others. If little boys are taught to despise all the things that girls are supposedly all about, then men will despise all the things that women are supposed to be all about. It's all so simplistic and obvious, isn't it, yet the cornballs still don't seem to have grasped this basic and fundamental truth. They still make little girls figures of derision for little boys by dressing them up in ridiculous frills and frippery which has to be 'kept clean' at the expense of the child's freedom of movement and which is a totally selfish parental indulgence to satisfy their own vanity, since small children have little or no interest in appearance until they come to understand that dressing up 'pleases the adults'. They still give little boys guns, war games and wham bam annuals and still encourage them to 'pretend' to kill. Christmas and birthday presents are still chosen by reason of gender and still encourage boys to be outgoing, inquisitive and creative, girls to be introvert, home-loving and intellectually undemanding.

At school, girls and boys are further divided right from the beginning, their identities polarised, their ambitions and expectations of themselves made to appear separate, their ideals opposing, their interests distinct. Partly this is done unconsciously, partly deliberately and partly as a means of control (divide and rule).

"Quiet now children. Group together in twos now, boys on the right, girls on the left (sic)"

or

"Boys take the blue bands, girls the red"

or

"Come on now you big strong boys, let's move these chairs and show the girls what you're made of". . .

. . . and so on. There is also a strong tendency for teachers either to turn a blind eye to unprovoked attacks by spiteful little boys or to applaud them for 'assertiveness', while the same behaviour by little girls is condemned as unnatural aggression.

When it is time to read, the parent instilled images of pretty, passive, intellectually defective and physically inferior girls and active, inquisitive and assertive boys are reinforced with pictures of little girls nursing dolls, sitting sewing, sitting knitting — and little boys driving tractors, playing cricket or being handed scalpels by obliging little girl nurses.

By the time the children reach the point at secondary school where, if fortunate, they may actually be given a CHOICE to do either needlework or woodwork, regardless of gender, the cornball messages will all have been thoroughly inculcated and it will be a brave girl who opts to do woodwork and an even braver boy who will take up needlework.[1] This proves to the cornball that boys and girls have natural proclivities towards certain activities, whereas all it really demonstrates is the power of social conditioning to lead people in pre-determined directions that are often contrary to their true desires and against their better judgement, for fear of ridicule.

By similar tactics girls and boys are encouraged to pursue different leisure interests and involve themselves in different sports. Girls are not encouraged (are, in the majority of cases, actively *DIS*couraged) to take up football or cricket, and those who protest are usually formed into 'girls' teams, which is totally unjustifiable and merely (as intended) diminishes their worth and shunts them into the familiar second class status reserved for women's activities.[2] There is absolutely *NO* reason why girls and women cannot play mixed-team football with boys and men providing, needless to say, that they are fit and active; there is no evidence that women *per se* have less stamina, are less accurate, or are less able to withstand a reasonable amount of rough and tumble and kicks on the shins than men. The familiar cornball argument against women joining men's cricket teams is that they wouldn't be able to face balls travelling at over a hundred miles an hour, but it seems to me that being hit by a ball travelling at that speed is going to do NOBODY any good, whatever their gender, and perhaps NOBODY should have to take that sort of risk in the name of sport, especially when just as much skill goes into spin and slow bowling and both can be just as effective as the brutish 100 m.p.h. delivery. Mixed sport could only improve it, it seems to me, by shifting the emphasis towards skill and away from brute force and intimidation. Nor is there any logical reason why

1. *Physical differences would in all probability always lead to an overall gender divide with activities such as needlework and heavy digging, but individual physical aptitude (which will frequently defy the 'norms' of gender) is not the same thing as the rigidly imposed divide of "Natural Occupations of the sexes", which is merely used as a means of undervaluing, socially and economically, women's contribution to society. 'Difference' should not mean 'Inferiority'.*
2. *Anybody who is inclined to doubt this may care to reflect on how many of the daily newspapers give day to day coverage of the results and performance of women's cricket, football, hockey or netball teams and how much time is allocated to them on television.*

boys should not play mixed-team netball and rounders, since they are only basketball and baseball under a different name. The reason for the reticence is obvious, and has nothing at all to do with consideration for women's supposed delicacy but is rooted in the fear that if women are seen doing EXACTLY the same thing alongside men they might prove to be just as good — an unpalatable thought for cornballs whose whole *raison d'être* rests upon their imagined superiority over women and whose pathetic little lives would shrivel away if the myth were finally exploded.

Manipulating sexual desire and gratification to fit into the patriarchal framework has proved, over the centuries, to be one of the most damaging and destructive practices of all for both sexes, but more disastrously so for women. The women's movement has made great strides towards altering the patriarchal bias against women's sexual needs and identity, but there is still a depressingly long way to go. Boys are STILL taught that sex is essential to their well being and that they should get it any way they can, by any devious practice at their disposal — while girls are exhorted to view their virginity as a prize and to dispense their favours with frugality, like handing out sweets to deserving children. As a result, men feel that since for them sex is a NECESSITY and for women is a mere INDULGENCE (if not an actual SIN), then the responsibility for avoiding unwanted pregnancies must necessarily be the woman's, not theirs. If a woman 'gives way' then it is her fault, her problem and no less than she deserves for her 'immorality' and 'lack of control'. Women learn to feel guilty about their sexual desires, and to suppress them for fear of falling foul of society's displeasure. Even if they defy the pressures and screw when they feel like it, they will still be plagued by guilt — especially if they are made pregnant. Girls and women who religiously (sic) follow the moral codes of the patriarchs to the letter will, more often than not, come to terms with their burgeoning sexual desires by convincing themselves that sex is dirty, ungodly and immoral, that all men are sex maniacs after their bodies and that it wouldn't be at all pleasurable, anyway. Such conviction is difficult to overcome and when the time comes, inside the sacred institution of marriage, for them to lower all the barriers and start to enjoy a sustained sexual relationship, most of these women find it impossible to keep up the pretence and if they are to avoid the despised label 'frigid' must spend a lifetime finding new excuses or grinding their teeth in resignation until 'it's over'. In fact, it should come as no surprise to ANYBODY that women are often incapable of enjoying sexual relations when the whole gamut of sexual imagery in our society is aimed at achieving male, rather than female, sexual arousal — the anomaly of which never ceases to astound me. Men, we are told, are more sexually active than women, more easily aroused, less in control of their sexuality. Now these assumptions may or may not have a grounding in reality but . . . if that is the case then why is it that WOMEN are expected to be the ones to attract, titillate and excite men, and not the other way round? Why are the advertising hoardings not filled with naked and sexy-looking men draped around cars and with sensual male tongues licking provocatively around ice creams? Why is page three of *The Sun* not dedicated to hairy chested macho men in suggestive poses and why are we not pursued up the escalator by visions of erected cocks, narrow male hips and tight little masculine arses? If men are indeed as sexually rampant and women as indifferent as we are led to believe Nature made them then surely all the excess of stimulation for the male parts that can be witnessed everywhere you turn your eye or tune your ear is creating an even WIDER state of sexual incompatability? If these assumptions are indeed true, then surely fashions should be centred around *MALE* adornment for the purpose of attracting and arousing the *FEMALE* and not vice versa? Something, somewhere, does not compute — unless "Female" is replaced by "Commodity" and "Male" by "Purchaser", and "Marriage" is viewed in the light of a financial transaction in the market place. It then becomes apparent that the goods must look attractive for the customer or he will go elsewhere, leaving the pretty doll to become soiled and chipped, left on the shelf without a place in the gentleman's lovely house and only a prayer away from destitution.

The outcome of any one of the different faces of

patriarchal bias in society's treatment of the sexes is predictably disastrous. Boys, after years of being told that girls are stupid, weak, boring and incapable are suddenly, aged fifteen, expected to view those same subjects of years of derision in the light of loving partners with whom they may share the rest of their lives. Early sexual relationships, with boys trying to 'get what they can' and girls attempting to hold out and give 'as little as possible' are a battleground of mind games, subterfuge, guilt and incomprehension. Girls want steady relationships in which sex may JUST be permissible, boys still want to be with other boys and 'get what they can WHEN they can'. Most early relationships are fraught with pain and bitterness, especially for girls. Many lead to unwanted pregnancies for a variety of reasons, but often because the girls, — who don't INTEND to have sex — don't use contraception because to do so outside a steady relationship (or outside marriage, depending on the extent of the brainwashing) is a pre-meditated admission of intention to 'give way', and many girls are too frightened/guilty/intimidated by social pressures to make such a blatant statement of intent; the boys take no precautions at all because they feel it is not their responsibility and the girls are usually too unsure of their ground to insist. In later years, when the initial physical attraction has worn off, men and women within marriage all too often find (surprise, surprise) that they are sharing a house with a person with whom they have absolutely nothing in common. She is emotional, in need of love; he is cold and restrained. She is home-loving, domestic, pre-occupied with demands of child and home; he is work orientated, non-domestic, pre-occupied with demands of business and finance. He comes home tired and wants to relax in the home, away from the pressures of the outside world; she wants to talk, go out, get away from the house and *into* the outside world. He wants to spend the weekend in the garden or watching male-dominated sports like football and cricket; she wants to go to jumble sales and DO things outside the home, *SHE* has no interest in men's football and cricket matches. Their sexual relations have long since become a matter of routine and obligation, or ceased altogether. They have nothing to talk to each other about, they have nothing in common. They are PERFECT opposites. PERFECT male and female stereotypes. He, having been brought up to admire strength, independence, capability and emotional restraint finds he cannot respect — often despises — the weak, clinging, dependent, incapable and simpering child-figure he calls his wife and cannot regard her as an equal being. He resents having to support her financially, resents her nagging and demands for affection. *SHE* is full of pain, resentment, loneliness and frustration, hates his callous disregard for her feelings, hates the way he never really listens to her, hates being dependent, longs for freedom, excitement, intellectual stimulation, sexual diversion. *SHE* reads romantic novels. *HE* reads The Economist. She reads her stars. He reads the sports page. Arguments ensue. He goes out, gets drunk, goes to football matches, goes away more and more 'on business'. They have affairs. They stay together for the sake of the children. They fight. She takes valium. They get divorced, etc. etc. Whatever else they do, they do NOT communicate. They do NOT like one another. They do NOT understand one another. They are not happy.

The point that cornballs don't seem able to grasp is that keeping women in their 'place' isn't just degrading to women, it also nourishes an acceptance of the whole concept of power and powerlessness, superior and inferior, master and servant, which in itself keeps a large percentage of the MALE population in a position of subservience to OTHER men. It keeps them working in poorly paid, soul-destroying jobs in abject fear of being equated with the ultimate symbols of powerlessness and weakness — WOMEN — and it allows even the most exploited and downtrodden of men to accept their lowly positions out of a misguided belief in their own superior status. (If they're not amongst the most powerful of men, at least they're not WOMEN). Add to this the fact that their domestic lives in the company of what they see as an inferior species are far from ecstatic, that their sexual relations are frequently unsatisfactory and that the 'masculine' (in direct opposition to the 'feminine') values that are thrust upon them to denote power and superiority are the very values that are threatening to destroy the world — and it makes you wonder why on *EARTH* anybody should wish to pass all this on to their hapless children. It is something that all those responsible for the welfare of children should think very hard about next time they are tempted to fall back on all those seemingly harmless platitudes and practices to which the cornball is so addicted.

4. ALL CREATURES GREAT AND SMALL

☆ *In 1978, five and a half million animal experiments were performed in the United Kingdom alone. About 229,500 of these were the animals which scientists are licensed to torture to death each year using the LD50 test. This test (lethal dose 50) is the method of establishing how poisonous a new chemical is to humans by feeding it to rats, rabbits, guinea pigs, birds, fish, monkeys and dogs in batches of 50-60 at a time, in ever increasing doses, until half of them are dead. Those still alive after one set of tests are destroyed or used again. None is permitted to survive.*
☆ *Richard Adams on the Canadian seal slaughter.*

To what use are the slaughtered seal pups put commercially? Primarily, of course, the sealers are after the soft, cream-coloured pelts, which the pups retain until they have been in the water and which are at their best when the pup is about three weeks old. The sealer drives off the nursing mother, batters the pup about the head with a heavy, spiked club known as a "HAKAPIK", turns the pup over on its back — often while it is still alive, as the films clearly show — slits it from anus to throat with a sharp knife and pulls off the pelt and layer of blubber immediately beneath it. This he drags away, leaving the female seal sniffing at the pup's remains.
☆ *An extract from 'The Jungle' by Upton Sinclair, taken from 'The Beast' magazine, Spring 1980.*

They had chains which they fastened about the leg of the nearest hog, and the other end of the chain they hooked into one of the rings upon the wheel. So, as the wheel turned, a hog was suddenly jerked off his feet and borne aloft.
At the same instant the ear was assailed by a most

terrifying shriek; the visitors started in alarm, the women turned pale and shrank back. The shriek was followed by another, louder and yet more agonising — for once started upon that journey, the hog never came back; at the top of the wheel he was shunted off upon a trolley and went sailing down the room. And meantime another was swung up, and then another, and another, until there was a double line of them, each dangling by a foot and kicking in frenzy — and squealing. The uproar was appalling, perilous to the ear drums; one feared there was too much sound for the room to hold — that the walls must give way or the ceiling crack. There were high squeals and low squeals, grunts and wails of agony; there would come a momentary lull, and then a fresh outburst, louder than ever, surging up to a deafening climax. It was too much for some of the visitors — the men would look at each other, laughing nervously, and the women would stand with hands clenched and the blood rushing to their faces, the tears starting in their eyes.

Meantime, heedless of all these things, the men upon the floor were going about their work. Neither squeal of hogs nor tears of visitors made any difference to them; one by one they hooked up the hogs and one by one with a swift stroke they slit their throats. There was a long line of hogs, with squeals and life blood ebbing away together; until at last each started again and vanished with a splash into a huge vat of boiling water.

It was all so very businesslike that one watched it fascinated. It was pork-making by machinery, pork-making by applied mathematics. And yet somehow the most matter-of-fact person could not help thinking of the hogs; they were so innocent, they came so very trustingly; and they were so very human in their protests — and so perfectly within their rights. They had done nothing to deserve it; and it was adding insult to injury, as the thing was done here, swinging them up in this cold-blooded, impersonal way, without a pretence at apology, without the homage of a tear. Now and then a visitor wept, to be sure, but this slaughtering machine ran on, visitors or no visitors. It was like some horrible crime, committed in a dungeon, all unseen and unheeded, buried out of sight and memory.

The attitude of cornballs towards the creatures with whom we share the earth is as ambivalent, contradictory and hypocritical as it is in every other direction. Oh yes, they love little pussy wussies and doggy woggies and they are in the forefront when it comes to vociferous condemnation of those who blow up horses, shoot police dogs and ill-treat kittens — but they are a lot less keen to voice their disapproval of the cruelty involved in animal experimentation, fox-hunting and factory farming. Animal experimentation, they say, is a 'necessary' evil, fox-hunting is perfectly forgivable because it keeps down the foxes and factory farming is the only way to feed a growing population. Anyway, they say, in their most ludicrous displays of self-righteous hypocrisy, who can worry about ANIMALS when half the world is starving? (Since when, I ask myself, have THEY given a damn about the starving millions of the world, and since when have THEY been so burnt out with sympathy and commiseration for the abundance of human misery within the present status quo that they have no tears left to shed for animals?)

This is what they SAY, but the truth is that gushing over the virtues of fluffy little pets and being *OUT*raged at their mistreatment is painless, whereas abhorrence of factory farming may involve some kind of sacrifice, and condemnation of fox-hunting or animal experimentation would inevitably lead to a clash with the establishment — neither of which is an appealing prospect for the habit-bound, appearance-conscious, egotistical cornball. It is easier by far to be spiteful about Greenpeace, Hunt Saboteurs and all those who are fighting to alleviate some of the needless misery inflicted on animals than it is to actually try to DO something about it, or at the very least to give support to those who do; easier to poke fun at vegetarians than to be faced with the uncomfortable decision to change their habits and *GIVE UP* something that they find pleasurable in the interests of another creature; infinitely preferable to view animal rights campaigners as loony lefties or unrealistic, misguided idealists who are lacking in the cornball worldly-wise insight into the drives and limits of human nature than be forced to re-appraise their own bigoted attitudes or to examine the selfish motives behind their own convictions. Easier by far to do absolutely NOTHING to alter the present status quo than to let their imaginations wander into dangerous areas of conscience, guilt and human compassion.

None of the arguments used by the cornballs to excuse their attitudes towards animals really holds any water if you bother to go into them in any depth. The argument that it is NECESSARY for animals to die in experiments in the interests of medicine is spurious for many reasons. For a start, it is untrue to say that most animals are used in this endeavour, since the vast majority of them die to test such things as fumes, pollutants, tobacco substitutes, petrol additives, paint sprays, pest-killers, preservatives, dyes and thousands of other chemicals which flood the market each year and bring no real benefit to humankind whatsoever — usually the reverse — but even those that DO die in the supposed interest of the human species are slaughtered, for the most part, unnecessarily. Firstly, experiments done on animals are notoriously unreliable when it comes to translating the results to human beings. Secondly, it is perfectly possible to do many of the experiments on laboratory-grown cultures with similar — and often superior — results, but those responsible consider it more expedient to waste the lives of sentient animals, many of which die in agony without even the courtesy of an anaesthetic. There is no way that it can be morally or ethically justifiable to treat living creatures, capable of feeling exactly the same pain and fear as our own species, with such callous disrespect, especially since most of our present day health problems are caused by human stupidity and could for the most part be eliminated by cleaning up the environment and paying more heed to living health-promoting life styles and it is unforgivable to make entirely blameless creatures suffer for our mistakes.

The arguments put up by the elitist, sherry-quaffing community for continuing their bloody ritual are no more credible or morally acceptable than those proffered, past and present, in favour of bull-fighting, bear-baiting, cock-fighting or hare-coursing and nobody but the insensitive cornball, clinging tenaciously to self-interests, could possibly treat them with anything but contempt. Nobody but a cornball could pretend that the terrible suffering caused to baby seals and their distraught mothers could ever be justified on ANY grounds. Nobody but a cornball could consider it "Chic" to wear fur coats or "Good taste" to flaunt ivory ornaments as symbols of support for the cruelty, pain and ultimate extinction that they signify for vast numbers of our fellow creatures.

The more squeamish of cornballs — usually women who don't have to keep up their male counterparts' pretence of 'macho insensitivity' in order to demonstrate masculine dominance over feminine sentimentality — will actually go along with much of my abhorrence for the aforementioned atrocities, but the stumbling block invariably comes with EATING the little darlings. It may not be entirely justifiable to blind rabbits in order to test detergent number three hundred and fifty but eating them is another matter entirely. Meat eating, contends the carnivorous cornball, is a *NECESSITY*; meat eating is *HEALTHY*; meat eating is *NUTRITIOUS*; meat production is the most *EFFICIENT* means of providing hungry people with first-class protein. Well I'm sorry to deprive the cornball of such cosy convictions but not one of those contentions is actually true.

a) Meat eating is an indulgence of a minority of the world's population, not a necessity. Millions of people, the world over, have been vegetarians for generations, with no ill effects.

b) The consumption of meat and dairy products is now largely accepted by nutritionists to play a role in such maladies as heart disease, allergies, obesity, hardening of the arteries, varicose veins, kidney ailments, ulcers and thrombosis. Nor is it unrealistic to suppose that the unprecedented outbreak of cancers in the last fifty years is connected, in part at least, to the methods employed in factory farming encompassing, as it does, the injection of hormones and a variety of substances to unnaturally fatten the animals in the interests of greater profits. To quote from "Food for a Future" by Jon Wynne-Tyson:—

As is widely known, domesticated animals suffer from innumerable diseases — not only from cancer but also from tuberculosis, contagious abortion, swine fever, foot and mouth, mastitis and a host of others — and it would be naive indeed to suppose that all diseased meat is detected and fed to our pets instead of to us. To what extent cancers can be attributed to these repellant facts of animal exploitation has yet to be confirmed, but the statistics are reason enough for concern.

I can think of no more compelling reason for abandoning carnivorous habits than to reflect that every time you chew on a piece of juicy meat you are quite possibly sucking on the blood of a diseased animal.

c) Meat is no more nutritious than plant produce, but a vegetarian diet does require a little more THOUGHT, initially, in order to obtain a good protein balance, because some plant foods have what have been termed 'limiting amino acids', and they have to be complemented by OTHER plant foods to make good the deficiency. This is not difficult, once the principle of using grains and beans together has been understood, however, and there are many books on the subject to assist the beginner who really wants to make the effort (the most famous being *"Diet for a small planet"* by Frances Moore Lappe). It is not true to say that meat is a "first class" protein and vegetable protein "second class", as is often quoted gleefully by the carnivore, but more accurate to say that meat is a 'complete' protein. However, the benefit obtained from a combination of the right vegetable matter is not only EQUAL to meat in protein quality, it is SUPERIOR nutritionally because it contains Vitamin C and roughage, both very necessary ingredients for good health.

d) Meat production is NOT the most efficient means of feeding a hungry world, it is the *LEAST* efficient, since it necessitates the extensive growing of crops in order to feed them to livestock from which we receive an absurdly small exchange. Much of this foodstuff has to be imported, often from countries least able to spare it. Japan and Western Europe together have about one sixth the population of the poor world, yet they import twenty percent more grain than all the underdeveloped nations taken together — to feed to livestock. In addition to this, four fifths of the world's agricultural land is used for feeding animals and only one fifth for feeding human beings direct. If all this land were used to grow plant foods (grains, pulses, vegetables) to feed humankind direct, the world food shortage could be eradicated, since an animal must consume seven plant calories in order to produce one calorie's worth of food for human consumption.

Breeding animals as food is a luxury of the affluent minority of the world — it would be impossible to feed the world on the meat-based, rich-world diet, but perfectly possible for everyone to eat WELL and HEALTHILY if the selfish rich were to adopt the perfectly adequate diet of the rest of the world (those of the rest of the world who can eat anything at all, that is).

The callous disregard for the feelings of animals meted out by the largely cornball element of society is not only undesirable and morally indefensible, it is also potentially dangerous, because it actively propagates the 'predator' mentality and influences not only the way human beings relate to animals but rubs off on the way they relate to one another. Meat eating fosters the notion that "Human beings (the hunters/males) are aggressive, competitive and savage" and are incapable of altering the blood-thirsty, predatory nature given to them by an angry (male) God. The eating of meat also necessitates the suppression of the compassionate regard for the fate of soft, appealing creatures like lambs and baby calves which is spontaneous in small children and which very often leads to mealtime confrontation when the child refuses to accept the parental double standards implicit in teaching them to 'love' animals while at the same time expecting them to eat them. If the child continues to eat meat then the lesson will have been learned that certain seemingly unacceptable practices can be made acceptable by a process of rationalization and that compassion, on occasions, must be set aside in the interests of being 'human'. The acceptance of such double standards — together with the excusal of such morally reprehensible practices as experimentation on animals on the grounds that they are less intelligent, come from a different species and are unable to complain or fight back — can (and does) lead to the rationalization of atrocities like Hiroshima, Auschwitz and My Lai; such suppression of compassion towards those of God's creatures that are somehow 'different', and therefore not worthy of respect, can seem to excuse the rape of women in 'foreign' lands, the subjugation of men and women of a different colour or creed and the exploitation of the (ostensibly) less intelligent members of our own species . . .

. . . at the very least it must be acknowledged that eating frogs legs that have been torn from their hapless bodies while fully conscious must do very little for the ailing soul of humankind, and I would have thought that this grotesque practice would have made even the gluttonous, self-interested cornball pause to consider whether perhaps even *ANIMALS* were not entitled to a little more consideration than this.

5. ENVIRONMENTAL NEMESIS

Insistence upon the necessity of maintaining a balance in life and living in harmony with both our own environment and the cosmos is a belief not confined to the metaphysical reflections of "a load of lentil-eating macrobiotic cranks", as the Cornballs are wont to scoff in their ignorance. It is, in reality, a concept that is based on rock-hard, down-to-earth, biological and scientific *FACT* — and one which the whole world would do well to take an interest in, since every one of the delicate balances on which the survival of life on our planet depends is in danger of being upset by the arrogance of some members of our species in imagining that they can 'beat' Nature and ignore the very laws that govern our continued existence.

One important balance is the climatic balance, and is dependent on the radiations of the sun, the emissions of the earth, the influence of the oceans and the impact of the ice caps. Incoming solar radiation, coupled with the earth's own reabsorption of the heat it gives off itself, more or less equals the amount of radiation blocked from the sun or sent from cloud and earth surfaces back into space. The heat generated in the centre of the earth flows towards the poles, and from them cooler air is drawn towards the centre. This protects the earth and its inhabitants from extremes of temperature. It is a very delicate balance and one which, if upset to even a very minor degree could modify overall temperatures by 2 degrees either way, and would be responsible for either another ice age or for the disappearance of the ice, leading to catastrophic over-heating — in other words, we could very easily either fry or freeze to death. This is not as unlikely as it may seem, and the effects of our present way of life on another of nature's balances, that of carbon dioxide, makes it an ever more probable eventuality. At present, there is a life supporting balance between the amount of carbon dioxide in the atmosphere — a natural bi-product of human respiration — and the amount taken in by plants or dissolved into the oceans — but this balance is in danger of being upset by the burning of fossil fuels, which release large amounts of carbon dioxide into the atmosphere. In normal amounts (0.3% of the total atmosphere) carbon dioxide plays a small but specialized part in the earth's heating system, by intercepting the earth's radiations and transmitting it back to the earth — the famed greenhouse effect. It appears, however, that the increased amount of carbon dioxide is in danger of upsetting the balance of this operation and, added to the vast deforestation activities throughout the world which are reducing the amounts of carbon dioxide absorbed by plant life, could mean that the overall increase in temperature of 2°C (and hence our time for frying in a vastly overheated greenhouse planet) could be looming uncomfortably close.

Emissions of dust and soot into the atmosphere in vast quantities could also lead to unsought-after consequences. Already the earth's cloud cover has increased, and the higher the altitude of the concentrations, the more lasting they become — and nobody knows the consequences of such alterations in the biosphere. If they eventually reduce the passage of the sun's radiation, they could lower the earth's temperature, whereas if they reflect back the earth's own emissions of heat they would reinforce the greenhouse effect. Either way, disaster would ensue. It also seems possible that emissions of nitrates and sulphates from supersonic aircraft can unite with the critical supply of ozone in the biosphere and endanger the planet's safety from radiation by effectively depleting the upper atmosphere of one of the essential elements at present operating to provide us with a radiation shield. Caution has been advocated by some scientists regarding the large scale development of supersonic travel for this reason — doubtless unheeded.

Then there is the critical function of the oceans, which every year comes closer and closer to being upset. The oceans, too, play a crucial role in the earth's temperature control, together with other essential functions. The oceans are responsible for cooling the tropics and taking warm currents to cold regions. Oceans provide the water vapour which is drawn up by the sun and falls on the earth as life-giving rain. Ocean water acts as the planet's filtering system whereby debris is dissolved, decomposed and transformed into life-supporting substances. The oceans are the means by which clean water is returned to us by evaporation and precipitation. It is a major provider of oxygen, released by its phytoplankton — a full quarter of all the oxygen we breathe is produced by these infinitessimal phytoplankton lying on the seas at the point where air and water meet. Without water's special qualities for holding heat, much of the earth would be uninhabitable. Yet for all that, our species is slowly polluting the oceans and impeding their work. Every day, our oxygen-giving, rain-providing, life-sustaining oceans are being deluged with the refuse of thousands of polluted rivers and lakes all over the world — the waste from the whole world's industry, agriculture and overcrowded cities. The oceans have become the whole world's sewer, even to the point of burdening them with radioactive waste which will remain dangerous for thousands of years to come. They receive the run-off from agricultural fertilizers, and pesticides like DDT are carried vast distances by the ocean currents, accumulating in fish en route and causing such far reaching effects as sea-birds producing unhatchable eggs thousands of miles from where the stuff was originally used. The miserable catalogue of abuses to our environment goes on and on. Acid rain, caused by emissions of sulphur dioxide from power stations combining with water in the atmosphere to form clouds of sulphuric acid to be discharged wherever the rain falls, was recently described as the most serious environmental issue facing Western industrial nations and has led to polluted water supplies, dead fish, damaged and stunted crops and seriously damaged forests. The possibilities of huge oil slicks rises all the time — with all the concomitant evils of pollution, fouled beaches, dead birds and fishes and impairment of the functioning of the oxygen-producing phytoplankton. Ruthless and unnecessary deforestation of large areas of the earth's surface in the name of 'Agri-business' deprives us of a necessary source of oxygen, together with a regulator of water supply and a maintainer of soil fertility. Much of what would otherwise have been fertile land has been turned into deserts and dust bowls by ruthlessly cutting down trees to provide vast acreage of land for grazing livestock. Much land has become uncultivable as a result of removing the natural protection afforded by trees for use in paper making, because the topsoil gets washed away by the rains and leaves the earth barren and infertile. Eventually it turns to desert.

Whichever way you look at it, all this can only add up to one thing for present and future inhabitants of the earth — trouble; and however much cornballs may close their eyes and ears and try to forget about them, the problems won't just go away. At present, most of the blame for the worst crimes against the environment can be laid fairly and squarely at the door of the rich nations, since it is our industrialised, consumer societies that demand ever-increasing numbers of consumer items and ever-increasing amounts of energy with which to run more and more energy-guzzling inventions (the private car being the prime offender), but since representatives and upholders of our lunatic system have now transported Westernised ideals of 'Good Living' all round the world, we cannot but assume that the whole world (the capitalist world, at least) is now aspiring to pollute the environment in exactly the same way. So what happens when EVERY child in the world expects to consume the same amount of resources throughout its lifetime as the MINIMUM that the rich world inhabitant expects as a kind of birthright? At the moment, the industrialized production of meat and poultry (factory farming) is said to be the equivalent of the waste from 800 million people, and this at a time when only a MINORITY of the people in the world eats meat on anything like a regular basis. What happens when EVERYBODY expects to eat meat, which the rich world inisists is a necessity for human survival? What happens when the whole world is producing the estimated 1,100 lbs of waste products for which each American citizen is responsible every year, and what happens when the whole WORLD is discharging poisons, at the same rate, into our life-giving oceans? Just how long will these oceans be able to cope with this added onslaught and still be able to maintain their life-giving function? Just how long will the earth's finite resources last if *ALL* the world starts to squander, misuse and abuse them at the same rate as the rich world does now? Yet this, seemingly, is the cornball capitalist's ridiculous, unthinking and dangerous goal — The American Dream of unlimited growth transported all round the world.

How much longer I wonder, must the world suffer this mindless, cornball lunacy before sanity is allowed to prevail? How much longer must we suffer this ridiculous and unworkable system — this system of conducting human affairs which relies upon an unending search for new markets, for ever more consumer items producing, inevitably, ever increasing amounts of waste and using ever increasing amounts of energy, and which depends heavily upon the MINORITY reaping its benefits? How much longer will the earth, the oceans, the biosphere and nature itself compensate for this arrogant and selfish imprudence? How long have we got left?

How long? Maybe not even the length of your children's lives.

SECTION THREE

THE CORNBALL ESTABLISHMENT

The cornball mentality is not a state of mind confined to the rich, but it is entirely the responsibility of the rich — the self-appointed administrators and rulers, — to maintain the established order which keeps them and their children living in the style to which they have become accustomed. Cornballs who do not come from upper class backgrounds (which includes all the striving middle classes, much as they like to believe they are superior) are mere puppets dancing to the tune of the upper-crust manipulators, doing upper-crust dirty work and killing themselves at earlier and earlier ages from heart attacks and other stress-related ailments, while their wives die of boredom and barbiturates. Cornballs from all income brackets are boring and objectionable but the rich variety are also dangerous, vicious, manipulative and knowingly exploitative — a thoroughly nasty bunch, and no mistake. How, then, do they ensure that they keep hold of what they have stolen without the risk of revolution? How do they keep the menials, the middle managers, and the trades union leaders (the vast majority of them) spending their whole lives working against their own (or their members') best interests to maintain the status quo for them? How is it that union leaders are now more interested in maintaining the capitalist/hierarchical aims of management than in pressing for socialism in the interests of the workers? How have those rich cornballs managed to do such a thorough job of indoctrination that not only has there not been a revolution but in a recent survey Margaret Thatcher, that mouthpiece of rich, cornball man who makes no bones at all about the fact that her policies are designed to keep the rich rich, the poor poor, the unemployed in penury and women in subservience — was generally 'admired for her guts'? Obviously not without considerable dedication to the cause: not without the power of 'The Cornball Establishment' to foster the myths, twist the truth and re-establish the hierarchy in each new generation for the benefit of their children.

And where better to start than with tender, young, impressionable minds?

Average income in Britain is £5,300 a year. The annual cost of sending a child to one of the older public schools is £4,000. Around 2.6 per cent of children go to public schools. For the elite professions public school background in the 1970's was as follows:

☆ Top civil service 62%
☆ High Court and appeal judges 80%
☆ Church of England Bishops 67%
☆ University heads and professors 33%
☆ Directors of clearing banks 80%
☆ Directors of major insurance companies 83%
☆ Conservative MPs 73%
☆ Conservative cabinet 78%
☆ Labour MPs 9%
☆ Labour cabinet 29%
☆ Top army officers 90%

World Bank 1980; Sampson 'New Anatomy of Britain'; Field 'Inequality in Britain'. Collated by A. Simpson.

From 'New Internationalist' July 1984.

1. FORMAL EDUCATION

The first, and singly most important and effective means of manipulation that the rich have at their disposal is school, and fee-paying education is invaluable to them in re-establishing the class barriers in each new generation. It is a means of instantly recognising 'their own' and at the same time lowering the expectations of those at state schools, who are being taught to take their place below them as their employees and drudges. The qualifications rat-race is an ingenious means of making everybody believe that they have an equal chance and leads the mind away from the reality — that it is **HOW AND WHERE** you get your qualifications and how much money has been spent on acquiring them that counts, not how many you get.

School is where one earns one's distinguishing marks by which one's peers will know one all one's life; the old school tie, the refined accn't, the codified upper class vocabularly and the strict rules of behaviour (clothes to wear/not wear and when, attitudes to adopt towards the plebs, where to live, what to buy/not buy, where and what to eat, furniture to have/not have, flowers to grow/not grow, where to go on holiday to meet the other bores, acceptable forms of entertainment, acceptable sports to participate in, acceptable animals to like/kill etc.). At the end of the education farce all the lessons should have been well learned, with each member slotted neatly into his or her designated pigeon hole, conditioned to follow the rules and stay in their class for the rest of their lives and not over-reach their expectations. By the end of their years at school the lower orders will have been made to believe that they are mindless, inferior beings who will automatically take up manual, physical labours and will not expect too much money for what they do — and so on up the scale, each one being neatly slotted according to background.

On hearing this, cornballs will undoubtedly begin to scoff and bluster and scratch around for all the rags to riches examples they can dredge up, but the truth of the matter is overwhelmingly evident — rich kids get the best jobs, poor kids get what's left — or no jobs at all. Anybody who is inclined to argue about this, and anybody who feels I am being biased and unrealistic, just think how many Lawyers, Doctors, Judges, Stockbrokers, Barristers, Politicians, Accountants, Financiers, Bankers, top Civil Servants, Media bosses, Managing Directors — and anyone else in highly paid, comfortable, *respected* employment you know with working class accents or backgrounds, and then reflect on how many Dustmen, Factory Workers, Porters, Labourers, Miners, Road Workers, Bus Drivers, Lavatory Cleaners — and anyone else in lowly paid, dirty, manual, boring and/or undesirable occupations you know who went to fee-paying schools and speak in upper class accn'ts.

School has acquired a reputation for being the place where children go to learn the three 'R's' and improve their minds, but it has a multitude of sinister purposes above and beyond that simple aim. In fact, I would say that the three 'R's' were quite a long way down on the list of priorities, and judging by the number of kids who come out of school illiterate and incapable of doing the most elementary mathematical calculations (like checking if they get the right change from the supermarket), I am not alone in this belief. In fact, formal education is an indispensable tool not only in indoctrinating the rules of class behaviour but also in instilling the attitudes necessary to support the established hierarchy and lend it credibility. To rich kids, this means learning to believe that their privileges are a natural, God-given right and that the poor are their natural inferiors. It means eradication of guilt and an acceptance of, coupled with a callous disregard for, human suffering. (You may have heard this referred to as the stiff upper lip.) It is about establishing the right to join the old boy network which will stand them is good stead for a lifetime in securing connections, employment and financial support. It teaches them that theirs in the Kingdom, the Power and the Glory for ever. It means reminding them that Noblesse Oblige (the rich man's burden) — because if it doesn't they may well lose their credibility as those chosen by God to receive her/his special favours on earth. (It should be noted that they are also taught that Noblesse only Obliges the bare minimum to keep them out of trouble and keep the natives from getting too restless.) It means learning to believe that they are the natural rulers and administrators, appointed by God. It means learning to accept that they are different people to the poor and whereas THEY couldn't live in poverty and destitution and whereas THEY would go insane being unemployed, homeless and penniless, the lower classes don't mind at all. In fact the plebs really enjoy being cold and hungry and it is, after all, the responsibility of the poor to make sacrifices in the interests of their superiors. All rich kids know that after a few years at public school.

While rich kids are learning to assume the attitude of arrogant pomposity and insensitivity we know so well as being the trademark of the rich, poor kids are learning to lower their expectations and accept the harsh rules of inequality. Formal education for the poor means learning to accept that they will be the ruled not the rulers, the workers not the employers, the respectful not the contemptuous, the servile not the served, the manual not the intellectual. It means learning to obey orders, to accept boring, meaningless work providing no interest and no satisfaction and to work fixed hours for a fixed pittance. It means learning to do as they're told without question and to leave management to the managers — who always know best. It means learning to accept humiliation without rebellion, poverty without complaint. It means learning to believe, without question, that the rich are their natural superiors.

Another important function of formal education is to prop up established beliefs and prejudices by a planned programme of biased interpretation (lies) and non-information. School History leads us to believe that the British Empire was built by enterprise, bravery and white superiority — and omits to mention the less acceptable motive of greed, or the amount of suffering that was caused by those glory-seeking conquistadores. The History books at school do not speak in such emotive terms as snatching land, stealing resources and slaughtering and subjugating the native people and when, now and again, they are forced to acknowledge the existence of slavery it is quickly glossed over in the greater interests of riches, glory, victory and naval supremacy. Irish History hardly warrants a mention up to 'O' Level and any political analysis of the causes when broaching, fleetingly, the sensitive subject of the poverty, hardship and starvation caused by the potato famine is studiously avoided. No mention is ever made about England's part in creating 'The Irish Problem' and you leave school at 16 bemused at the whole situation and believing that the Irish Problem is somehow entirely the fault of the Irish people and feel no further need to dwell on the subject. Incredible amounts of time are wasted on the Monarchy, as though we should all see our lives and our History in terms of which Royal Family was plundering the riches and draining the energies of the nation at any given time. Social History is sorely neglected prior to higher education and there is precious little attempt at correlation between present world problems and History. The workability/desirability of capitalism is never questioned and no alternative system is ever discussed in any detail. George Orwell's *"Animal Farm"* is used as a blanket condemnation of all that is 'left' and interpreted as an illustration of the non-workability of all socialist systems on account of the demon human nature — in place of a warning to socialists against merely substituting one centralized power structure with another, which I'm sure was Orwell's intention. No attempt is made to familiarize the pre higher education pupil with current issues like feminism, environmental issues, third world problems or the peace movement and things that are of vital importance to a democracy, like extensive discussions of (party) politics so that everybody understands what the various parties are saying and can participate intelligently and informatively in the decisions which will affect their lives, are totally ignored. No attempt is made to give the child any understanding of world economics; and the causes of things that affect their lives in a very personal way, like recessions, unemployment and inflation, remain a complete mystery to most kids — as though only the GOVERNMENT has the right to have access to such secrets and as though the masses cannot be trusted with such highly important information.

Another manipulative side of our education system is in the pretence that males and females have 'equal opportunities', which is a cunning untruth when 'education' is overwhelmingly concerned with fitting its charges into a male-dominated system of production and economic expansion. The female, in this arena, is at an immediate disadvantage because, unlike the male, her responsibilities are considered to be two-fold — both productive *AND RE*-productive. School, however, does not admit to this obvious social reality and treats the female as though she were as free to pursue her ambitions in the 'productive' world as her male counterpart. What she is ACTUALLY told is:—

> Here is the means by which you can earn for yourself in *paid* productive work, a measure of independence *IF* you can fit it in with your *unpaid* duties to your husband, home and children or *IF* you are prepared to forfeit motherhood altogether.

The necessary and important reproductive and nurturing duties of humankind are not considered worthy of serious consideration in the school curriculum (unless it is exclusively a girl's school) and children are not encouraged to explore the possibilities of alternative life styles which may encompass the community care of children and which can be self-reliant and self-sufficient. The desirability of the patriarchal nuclear family — the 'consumer' unit — in which mother and children are cooped up for protracted periods while hubby goes out into the world and *PRODUCES*, is never seriously questioned in the classroom. Life after school, to the present education system, means production, expansion, economics and profit and has little or nothing to do with meeting human needs or finding out what could actually make children HAPPY in later years. What human beings actually 'need' is to subsist in reasonable comfort in congenial, healthy surroundings within a helpful community, to have the freedom to indulge their artistic and intellectual capacity to the full and to exchange ideas and emotions with others. All the rest, all the excess 'production' for which we have to suffer the division of labour, the subjugation of women and all the associated misery of a frantic, consumer society, is used to feed the greed of a small minority, not to enhance the lives of the large majority. The small minority, however, is in charge of our education system.

The amount of information that children are NOT given at school is quite staggering. Anything that could be useful to them in forming their own opinions, participating in their own destiny or protesting against the injustice inherent in the present status quo is withheld from them. Any chance they may have of taking control of their lives and living them in their own way and in their own interests is removed by crushing their self-confidence and teaching them to be dependent on established practices and a paternalistic government (a 'guided' democracy). Truth about past events is twisted and doctored out of all recognition and any hopes the youngsters may have about making positive steps towards establishing a humane and egalitarian society are trampled underfoot by the weight of establishment indoctrination, lies and non-information. The reason for all this is, of course, that those in control — those with the money, the power and the privileges — don't want too many people to start thinking for themselves and discussing alternatives, because it is obviously more difficult to manipulate informed people. The result is that the majority of people in this country are extremely naive in their political analysis and a horrifying percentage of the population quite happily admits to 'not understanding politics', while many more select their political candidates on the basis of who their parents voted for or because they look nice, sound convincing or have nice smiles. Margaret Thatcher won the vote of the British people on her Iron Lady image and the fact that she believed in STRONG government; yet anybody who bothered to ask what STRONG actually means in governmental terms would have to concede that it means *DICTATORIAL* — the very antithesis of the free democracy the British people profess to be so vehemently determined to defend against totalitarianism and dictatorship. It is frightening how easily the politicians are able to get away with such cheap tricks and how readily some people will part with their individual freedom in order to bathe in the fragile light of a dictator's reflected glory.

Of course, background also plays a part in children's conditioning and undoubtedly has its effects on their development and the extent of their scholastic achievement, and of course school cannot be blamed for ALL society's failings — but it plays a VERY large part in propping up the status quo and re-establishing the hierarchy of privilege, class and patriarchal dominance. Of course children will never have equality all the while we have an unequal society — but for as long as our children are made to suffer the repressive and humiliating experience of institutionalized education at all, the abolition of fee-paying education to ensure that ALL children at least received the SAME[1] schooling would be a big step in the right direction. Perhaps under those conditions the quality of the schooling itself would improve and there would be more emphasis on information rather than on *MIS*information and *NON*-information; and it would also remove one very convenient means by which the elite at present trains the next generation of elite to assume power and safeguard its privileges.

2. THE MEDIA

Education takes care of many of the threats to their wealth and power that the rich might otherwise encounter, but there is always that underlying fear of rebellion from the ranks in later life so it is necessary to have some means of keeping up the pressure and ensuring the natives don't become too well informed. The Media could be a tremendous headache to them or a great asset, and since they own most of the daily newspapers and are in most of the top administrative/decision making/policy making positions in television and radio, they make sure it is used as an asset. The fact that we live under a system we are pleased to call a democracy means that they have to try a bit harder than they would if we lived under a self-confessed dictatorship because they have to create the illusion of such

1. *I should say in passing that if "same" means continuing to fix the priorities of education around feeding the requirements of competitive industry then women will remain the 'second sex' in a society dominated largely by men, since women's time-consuming reproductive functions will inevitably hamper them in a cut-throat, competitive world. Likewise, if a major role of education continues to be the pursuit of minority excellence then the majority will still be subordinated and we shall remain a divided society — a majority of spectators bowing in humble reverence to the achievements of the few and its inevitable bed-partner — a subjugated majority ruled by the whims of a powerful minority.*

things as equality, liberty, choice, equity and social concern, so television and newspapers have to appear to give a choice, be balanced, present both sides of the story. In fact, *ALL* the daily newspapers, with the possible exception, on occasion, of *The Guardian* and *The Mirror*, say exactly the same things but from slightly different angles and in different language, according to which class they are aiming at — and I wouldn't go so far as to call the two exceptions 'alternatives'. Television presents a balanced point of view by saying:—

"Will you go to bed WITH your teddy bear or WITHOUT it?"

In other words, a *controlled* alternative with a single end in view. Live discussions of current affairs are often limited by the kind of people involved in them (no articulate left-wing celebrities like pop or film stars and no working class heroes who might influence young and/or working class minds and get them interested in the issues — seldom a black face, seldom a feminist, seldom anything other than representatives of the middle classes) and the format of the programmes is often organised so that the alternative arguments are pre-determined. For example, discussions about employment invariably revolve around such considerations as:—

How to protect jobs and give workers a living wage	versus	How to be competitive, make profits and expand the economy

and are usually discussed between right-wing or middle-of-the-road (same thing) union leaders and right-wing or middle-of-the-road employers. Nobody amongst this self-interested bunch ever raises the question "Why do we *HAVE* to be competitive, why do we *HAVE* to make profits, why does the economy *HAVE* to expand? In whose interests are we having to 'cut down labour costs, become more competitive, make greater and greater profits'? Why can't *MANAGEMENT* forfeit some of their profits and fabulous salaries, cut back on their company cars, perks, hidden assets, tax dodges, cheap mortgages, expense accounts, free health insurance, free private education for their children etc. etc.?"

Television and radio discussions about unemployment

revolve around how to cut down unemployment or prevent it from reaching the six million mark, not about how to re-organise the system so that unemployment doesn't exist — so that, in other words, there are no such things as employERS and employEES and so that nobody has to be dependent for their livelihood upon market forces, economics, recessions, and the continuing increased profits of a minority. Documentaries about poverty studiously avoid painful comparisons with the extravagant life styles of the rich and avoid any political analysis or questions about the morality of a society that allows such appalling inequalities to exist. They usually just end up tamely and pathetically whining "Isn't it awful, but what is the answer, given that capitalism is beyond criticism?" and the answer they come up with, given that they are totally unprepared to discuss the root causes of the problem and attack the capitalist system and the greed of the minority in whose interests it all has to continue, is that there *IS* no solution. They always avoid saying anything that might risk making people ANGRY about the greed of the rich and REBELLIOUS about their own poverty and underprivilege. They never condone the righteous anger of the poor, never admit that they would be perfectly justified in feeling furious at being the victims of a grave injustice, *NEVER* suggest that many of our oppressive laws are *BAD* laws that should be ignored and never *EVER* make suggestions about taking community action to change the situation — that, after all, would be showing political bias. It would, undeniably, be showing a bias against the upholders and beneficiaries of privilege, and since those are the very people who are running the show it would undoubtedly be very painful for them to be so biased.

However much you may be persuaded you are being given a choice and are making up your own mind about current issues, you are in fact being pressured to believe and uphold the following principles:—

1. Right-wing is BRITISH, left-wing is COMMUNIST. Right is good, left is bad

2. The Monarchy is a necessary part of a 'free' society

3. Trades unions are trying to bring the country down

4. Capitalism is the ONLY system with right on its side. Freedom equals conservative (small 'c' openly, capital 'C' tacitly)
5. We must RESPECT Royalty and the upper class
6. Upper class accents equal intelligence. Working class accents equal stupidity.
7. Management works in the interests of the people, trades unions and lefties work in the 'selfish' interests of socialism. (sic)
8. The British are ALWAYS right.

The news invariably portrays strikers as 'unreasonable, irresponsible, selfish and bent on bringing the country to its knees'. Any shots of strikers are especially chosen to leave an impression of rowdiness, violence and disruption. You are never given THEIR point of view unless it comes through a union representative (as though the workers are too stupid to express their own opinions) and never hear what THEIR grievances are in any depth, only the management viewpoint and the repressive outlook of right-wing television editors and producers. You only hear what the strike is doing to the 'country', which really means how it is threatening to affect management pockets. In the health workers dispute it was never the workers' grievances which were given all the publicity but the *EFFECTS* of the strike. Likewise with the water workers; we didn't hear how difficult it was for THEM to exist on their meagre wages or *WHY* they were on strike, only what effects their irresponsible actions were having on the public. How, I wonder, would those exploitative rich men who earn hundreds of pounds for a few hours work like to live on the money the average manual worker gets? Would THEY go on strike, I wonder? But then these are the kind of questions that are never asked. They keep their rises, their perks, their phenomenal and ridiculous salaries VERY quiet. When we talk about workers bringing the country down we are (the Media is) talking about the manual worker who wants an extra £4 per week, not the executive who, at a single stroke, gets a rise of £5,000 and upwards a year. The news is the news that rich men want you to hear and from the viewpoint they want you to see it. Wars that the news-makers cannot use to attack communism or the left wing are virtually ignored; we don't hear too much about El Salvador or any other peoples' revolts all over Latin America and Africa, because the political implications of them are too difficult and painful for the right wing to explore — or allow we the viewers to explore — whereas Afghanistan was an eagerly grasped opportunity to attack the repressive nature of Soviet communism while drawing tacit and ridiculous parallels with the left wing in this country. When reporting on the tribulations of the workers' trades union 'Solidarnosc' in Poland the emphasis was placed heavily on Soviet repression, at exactly the same time as Thatcher's government was making vicious and concerted attacks against the union powers in this country — but they didn't comment on this and no such parallels were drawn. It is an indication of the contempt in which they hold the British public and of the amount of confidence they have in their own powers of manipulation that they could assume (quite rightly it seems, in the light of subsequent events) that the British public would not draw those parallels either.

If the news were to tell the truth about the peoples' revolt in El Salvador it would have to report that:

"The people of El Salvador are losing their battle against the oppression and inequality of their society and are being murdered in their thousands by vicious government goon squads using foreign arms, foreign money and foreign expertise" (I leave you to imagine whose)

Instead, when the revolt is not ignored altogether we hear that:

"Government troops are suffering losses but are managing to keep the guerrilla attacks under control".

In other words the rich are under attack but are managing to hang on to their riches with the help of a well indoctrinated military. If we were to be told the truth about the American involvement in Nicaragua it would be that yet again 'Big Brother America' is poking its nose where it doesn't belong in order to bully the Nicaraguan people and their people's government into re-instating a Hitlerite dictatorship acceptable to the USA, to enable them to move in their multi-national companies and exploit the country's labour and resources in their own interests and to the detriment of the majority of the inhabitants. News-makers should be lamenting the fact that this brave little country — whose people had the considerable courage to stand up against the vicious and repressive Somoza dictatorship and win their freedom from a cruel and merciless regime — is now being threatened, by an outside power, with being hurled back into the jaws of fascism. But of course, our news-makers do no such thing — any more than they did for Chile or Vietnam. Our news-makers gleefully dance to the tune of right-wing imperialism, applaud its bully-boy tactics and lie through their teeth, along with America, about 'communist threats' and 'defence of freedom' — and Nicaragua, like Chile, will eventually be sacrificed on the altar of the rich and powerful — the altar of greed — without a tear having been shed for them. On the contrary, we will all be encouraged to join with the Americans in singing the Star Spangled Banner and to give three cheers for the victory of freedom over tyranny. If it weren't so tragic it would be funny.

The right-wing press runs on exactly the same kind of principles, works just as hard to keep the public ill-informed and is just as unprepared to criticize the capitalist system or suggest any worthwhile changes. The anger and frustration caused to the lowly-paid and unemployed by their constant humiliation at their powerlessness to alter their circumstances — which SHOULD be directed against those who *PUT* them in that position and who strive so hard to keep them there — is channelled into an unreasoning, blood-spitting hatred against a multitude of scapegoats from the IRA, homosexuals, petty thieves, muggers, drug-pushers and users, 'scroungers', strikers and the left wing right through to French lorry drivers and football hooligans. No opportunity is passed up to attack and discredit the Women's Movement, CND, The Animal Rights Movement, The Ecology Movement, The Gay Rights Movement, Greenpeace — you name it, if it talks about other people's/creature's 'rights', or any way threatens to try to change things for the better, the right-wing press, en masse, attacks it, ridicules it and discredits it.

The gutter press is a dumping ground for the overspill of human outrage — the part that might be dangerous if it were not de-fused and directed away from the guilty parties. Anything that threatens rich men's profits and upper class privileges, or attempts to give other people a better deal (ultimately, of course, at their expense) is crushed underfoot at the first opportunity. Middle class papers like *The Express* and *The Daily Mail* play on middle class snobbery and holier-than-thou morality to convey their messages, while *The Sun* relies on the Royal Family, page three tits and working class fears to instil racism, sexism and respect for their richer and betters into the lower income classes. They all rely heavily on cornball prejudice and all use the threat of socialism/communism as a whip to beat up reactionary outcries; and none of the cornball readership seems to take time off to ask "why have we all got this paranoid fear of socialism and the left wing, and why are all these newspapers so anxious to keep us away from them?" They all work very hard (especially *The Sun*) to divide the working class and set them fighting amongst themselves, spying on one another and condemning one another for trying to fight back. They set black against white, men against women, north against south, worker against worker. The worker who buys his council house and reads *The Mail* is encouraged to become a middle class snob and look down on the worker next door who rents his council house and reads *The Mirror*. Workers are chivvied into accusing each other of 'scrounging' and the latest ploy is for us all to spy on our peers in case they may be plotting to commit a crime. Feminists are the butt of all the media's venomous humour and women who try to get equal pay and equal treatment are ridiculed and discouraged. Racism, if not openly encouraged, is certainly not *DIS*couraged, which it needs to be if old prejudices are to be disproved and outlawed. The British flag is waved and supported via an unholy obsession with the Royals and whenever Britain is involved in an international issue the cornball press makes a huge, concerted effort to rally its cornball readers in support — regardless of whether we are right or wrong and with *NO* concessions made towards reporting the other side of the story.

Both television and the right-wing press vehemently deny that they are biased and none would admit to working solely in the interests of the rich — yet by upholding the status quo and resisting any attempts at change it should be patently obvious even to the thickest of cornballs that this is *EXACTLY* what they do. Since the status quo is a state of inequality, the media would need POSITIVELY to discriminate AGAINST the situation if it were to act in anybody else's primary interests other than the established upper class — and since it has proved itself totally unprepared to do this it must admit to being *POSITIVELY IN FAVOUR* of inequality. This, of course, should come as no surprise when you consider who are the people who run the Media, because they are quite obviously amongst those who would stand to lose most if the present state of inequality was rectified. It is difficult to see, however, what the rest of the cornball population thinks it can gain by letting them get away with it.

3. THE LAW

Saying that the Law exists primarily to protect the life style and property of rich, upper class, white men will no doubt send cornballs into apoplectic seizures, but it is difficult to deny that these are the people who invariably benefit from its effects. They are certainly not the ones to suffer.

If Baron and Baroness Tory live on an estate of 100 acres and leave this to their son, Lord Fauntleroy, when they die, this is not considered theft, yet the distinguished Lord has done nothing whatever to earn all that land, which belongs to humankind. He has stolen it for his own use and deprived the rest of the population of its benefits. He will not, however, be prosecuted.

If Pete Smith appropriates a transistor radio from Lord Fauntleroy's Rolls it is called theft, and if he has been guilty of previous such aberrations from the Law he will no doubt be locked up as a menace to society.

If Lord Fauntleroy employs Pete Smith as a cashier in one of his many supermarkets and pays him £60 per week, while he himself makes a profit of some £60 per day (a conservative estimate) out of his labour, this is not called theft, he will not be considered guilty of any crime and he will not be prosecuted. On the contrary, it was probably the means by which he obtained his title. If Pete Smith takes it on himself to redress the balance a little he will find himself in court, frowned upon by a deeply disapproving and distinguished member of the upper class.

In the last century it was legal for rich landowners to put man traps on their estates to protect their stocks of game from poachers and many of the poor wretches caught in these appalling contraptions, who were often starving and trying to feed a starving family, sustained dreadful injuries. It was also a hanging offence to steal a sheep, as it was for pickpockets (a theft of as little as 5 shillings would secure the death penalty). Striking was illegal and the Corn Laws, which protected the profits of the land owning (ruling) class by keeping the price of corn artificially high, caused great hardship and frequent starvation to the poor. When, in 1830, starving field labourers rioted in support of a demand for half-a-crown a day, three were hanged and 420 were deported to Australia.

It is easy to see the inhumanity in these laws and easy to see in whose interests they worked. Most people today would not deny that they were cruel, barbarous and the result of the selfishness of the rich. Yet these laws were not changed without pain and struggle, and the people who changed them were quite definitely NOT the cornballs of the time and most definitely not the rich, who fought tooth and nail against anything which seemed to threaten their privileged life-style. (When Samuel Romilly tried to repeal the death penalty for the theft of five shillings, he was regularly defeated by the House of Lords.) Here in the 1980's the same principles still apply; the laws still protect the property of the rich, still protect their rights of inheritance and still protect their wealth and profits to the detriment of the rest of the community. Only the severity of the punishment has changed, not the rules by which the poor are expected to abide under *threat* of punishment. It is easy to see how the Law Lords of the last century would today be consumed by moral outrage at the suggestion of abolishing the rights of inheritance or making it illegal to make profits from the labours of others — and just as easy to imagine those of today fighting tooth and nail against repealing the inhuman laws of the last century. Only by the concerted efforts of concerned people who are prepared to seriously criticize what is going on around them does anything ever get changed or improved — then as now. The social philanthropists of the last century, such as Robert Owen, to a small extent forced the ruling class to take some interest in, and responsibility for, the living standards of the people from whom it had stolen the resources of the land and on whose labour it parasitically fed. Laws were passed which protected people, to a small degree, from the more outrageous forms of exploitation practised by the wealthy. The Factory Acts limited the hours children under 13 could slave in a facory to 9 per day, and for any person under the age of 18 to 69 hours per week. Even then, reforms that are conceded as a gracious gift from the ruling class in an atmosphere of 'Noblesse Oblige' and which do not seriously affect the wealth and life style of those who bestow them are of limited value. Lasting benefits that go some way towards altering the balance of power or making the rich more accountable for their actions — like universal suffrage and trades unions — are always etched in blood and have to be wrenched from the self-interested rulers by threats, violence, demonstrations and social uprising. Polite requests for relief from hardship and injustice never softened hard and selfish hearts, and nothing was ever changed by working class cornball reactionaries clinging to 'what has always been' in the faint-hearted belief that one day, out of the goodness of their gentlemanly and ladylike hearts, the rich will allow the meek to inherit the earth.

Women's problems within the law have traditionally sprung from the assumption that they are the property of men (much as the poor are considered to be the property of the rich) to do with as men think fit, and such freedoms as women now have have been painfully won and grudgingly conceded. Rape is difficult to prove and women are deterred from reporting it through the scepticism they meet with from the police coupled with humiliating examinations and gruelling interrogations — often carried out by men. Men are still forgiven on the slightest pretext and women are still portrayed as the villains in the true, British tradition of blaming the victim and making no attempt to establish the causes of the crime or who are the *true* villains. Rape within marriage is not recognised as a crime since the woman is considered to have agreed to certain 'obligations' when she took the vows of marriage, and subsequently relinquished her right to refuse. Battered wives are commonplace, but the police tend to view this as 'a domestic affair' i.e. the husband's right to do with the goods as he pleases, not a crime against human rights. The law protects men against women — against women's demands, women's rights and women's freedom to alter their destiny or free themselves from the demands of men — and this is no more clearly demonstrated than by the ludicrous laws of prostitution, which state that it is illegal for a prostitute to solicit, but legal to give the service if the customer requests it. In effect this means a man can approach, harass and make lewd suggestions to a shop-girl on her way home on the pretext of believing her to be a prostitute, and she will have to prove her innocence of soliciting rather than he his innocence of harassment. She is automatically the assumed criminal, guilty until proven innocent, as she has been branded in patriarchal religious imagery since the time Eve supposedly unleashed evil on the world and made cornball man into the obnoxious, war-mongering little creep that he is today. One cannot help reflecting that it is high time he took responsibility himself for his nastier habits and lack of self-control, rather than always trying to blame women for encouraging him to display them.

Legislation for equal pay and the anti-discrimination Bill, together with the Corrie Bill against women's right to choose whether or not to have children, are still sufficiently recent to recall the struggle and the tenacious clinging of the cornballs to the traditional patriarchal status quo, and the Abortion Act was met by unreasoning, venomous accusations — the underlying messages of which rang loud and clear:—

'God is a man and if he says a woman should be pregnant, she should stay pregnant'

'Women are bearers of SONS, *so if she has an abortion she is taking* HIS *life and* HE *must be protected at all costs'*

'How can men be expected to control women, the slaves of nature, if they start controlling their own destinies and making decisions for themselves? The next thing is they'll be trying to control MEN'

'Women are nasty, dirty, promiscuous bags and hussies who flaunt themselves in front of men and get themselves pregnant. If they have sex they must take the consequences. Men aren't responsible for their urges, it's all WOMEN'S fault for giving way'

'MAN decides when WOMAN has babies, and that's all there is to it'

Apart from the letter of the law, the machinery and spirit of it is biased against the less privileged members of society — the poor, women and non-whites. Taking someone to court to try to get justice for a grievance like (1) unfair dismissal from work, (2) harassment of women by male employers leading to the women having to leave their jobs, (3) harassment of, or threats to, women by ex-husbands or lovers, or (4) unfair dismissal from work on the grounds of colour — or any other nasty little prejudice — is a long and tedious process and legal aid is not always easy to come by. Many people give up trying to fight large organisations in despair at the number of obstacles placed in their way and there is the added disincentive to individuals that if they cannot get legal aid and lose the case they may be placed in real financial difficulty trying to meet the legal costs. Large concerns, private and public, can afford to take the chance on losing a case, the individual often cannot — especially the poor, women (who are often dependants) and non-whites, who are usually among the poorest members of the community and often have difficulty with the language, the customs and the procedures to follow, not to mention the hostility and lack of co-operation they often encounter from police and officials. Added to this, the people who are involved with upholding the Law and meting out justice are, overwhelmingly, white, male and middle or upper class, with the possible exception of the police who seem to harbour a high percentage of thugs from a variety of backgrounds. Women and non-whites are not well represented at the bar and I have yet to encounter a black woman with a cockney accent sitting in Solomon's chair under a Persil white wig, so any sympathy for working class/black miscreants — who are the ones who most often find themselves in court — is bound to be limited, while the judgement in rape cases appears more frequently to be directed against the victim than against the alleged aggressor.

(Why did you place yourself in a position where you could be raped? What were you DOING out after ten o'clock at night trying to tempt men into raping you? Why did you GO to his room and put the poor, demented little man under intolerable pressure to rape you, beat you up and leave you for dead with a broom handle rammed up your cunt? You are an unbelievably irresponsible young woman and deserved all you got, if I only had the power I would send you and all the other little sluts like you to prison for life, away from decent male citizens.)

Judges are usually portrayed as being rather backward, upper class twits who don't understand the prisoner's jargon,

'Um . . . excuse me Mr. Jackson, but what exactly IS a bunch of fives . . .

but who, underneath it all, know EXACTLY what the score is. The fact is, it is much more likely that they are just upper class twits who really DON'T know. How WOULD they understand the pressures that make the poor, the underprivileged and the social misfit commit crimes? How would they, who have been sheltered, protected and pampered all their lives from the day they were born have any notion of the state of mind of someone who has had nothing but hardship and disillusionment all their life? How could they, who were born to be respected, know how it feels to live your whole life in fear of being humiliated, degraded and sneered at by the likes of THEM just because of your sex, your colour, your background or the way you talk? How could they, who have never ever had to worry about the mortgage, the gas bill, where the next meal for the kids is coming from or whether they will ever get another job begin to know what despair is like? What makes them believe that they, who have been given all the fruits of humankind's blood and sweat and tears as a birthright, have the right to sit in pious judgement over those they have cheated out of everything down to their last vestige of human dignity? The answer is that they DON'T, on all counts. The nobility used to make a great

fuss about being tried by their peers in the House of Lords
if they got caught out in some underhand practice, no
doubt because they felt that their chances of receiving
justice were more realistic if they were judged by people
who understood them, came from similar backgrounds and
were of like minds and cultural understanding. It is a pity
the same considerations could not be extended to the rest
of the community.

The Law, say its cornball defenders, is an instrument of
the "State" by which order is maintained for the benefit of
the "People" — but for this contention to have any
meaning we must first determine what is meant by the
"State" and who, exactly, are the people it supposedly
protects through the Law. Since, by dint of this claim,
there is an obvious distinction being made between "State"
and "People" it appears that there are those who consider
themselves law-makers by some invisible divine mandate
and others who must be content to abide by their rules. So
what is this exclusive body that constitutes the "State" for
the purposes of Law and Order? Presumably it must be the
Government. Who, then, are the "People"? Well, as I've
gone to some pains to illustrate, the Law does very little
when it comes to protecting the rights of women, the poor
or ethnic and minority groups, nor is it especially
sympathetic to the rights of homosexuals. In recent times
the Law has intervened to take away the trades union
rights of public sector workers, prevented workers picketing,
gaoled strikers and restricted workers' freedom of movement.
It does not, therefore, operate in the best interests of
workers. So all in all, there aren't too many "People" left
who can feel secure in the 'protection' of the Law and it
seems to me that it would be more realistic to say that the
Law is an instrument of the State to protect itself
AGAINST the people, which can be quite adequately
illustrated by the following examples of current British
Law (abridged).

OFFENCES AGAINST THE STATE

1. Treason

*Treason means treachery. It is betraying or breach of faith
and in Law denotes the grave crime of treachery towards*

the sovereign as head of the State or ANY BETRAYING OF THE STATE ITSELF.[1]

Treason is a most serious crime, being directed against the security of the State, and is punishable on conviction by death.

2. Sedition *(Some striking miners were recently charged with this)*

Sedition is a general term covering attempts to excite discontent or disaffection, disorder or tumult, or to subvert the Government, constitution or Laws of the country.

Sedition, being against the safety of the State, is an offence at common law.

Sedition consists of acts, writings or conduct which do not amount to treason, but which must be punished in the interests of the State, for if unchecked, sedition leads to disorder, and possibly to revolution. It is a crime against society nearly allied to that of treason.

A writing of a seditious nature is known as seditious libel and the writer CANNOT PLEAD THE TRUTH OF HIS LIBEL AS AN EXCUSE FOR PUBLISHING IT.

A speaker at a meeting who has used seditious words may be indicted for his seditious speech and the circumstances of the meeting itself may render the meeting an unlawful assembly.

3. Prevention of Terrorism (Temporary Provisions) Act 1976

Any person commits an offence who a) belongs or professes to belong to a proscribed organization, b) solicits or invites financial or other support for a proscribed organization, or knowingly makes or receives any contribution in money or otherwise to the resources of a proscribed organization, or c) arranges or assists in the arrangement or management of, or addresses, any meeting of 3 or more persons (whether or not it is a meeting to which the public are admitted) knowing that the meeting is to support, or to further the activities of, a proscribed organization, or is to be addressed by a person belonging or professing to belong, to a proscribed organization. The

1. *All emphasis is mine.*

organizations so far proscribed are the Irish Republican Army and the Irish National Liberation Army.

4. Official Secrets Act

Deals with spying and other practices prejudicial to the safety or interests of the State.

It is an offence for any purpose prejudicial to the safety or interests of the State to approach, inspect or enter any prohibited place or to make any sketch, model or note likely to be of any use to an enemy (including a POTENTIAL *enemy).*

It is an offence to retain for any purpose prejudicial to the safety or interests of the State any official document, or to fail to comply with any direction respecting same.

It is an offence to communicate to any other person any official information issued for one's own use alone, or without lawful authority, to have in possession official information issued for the use of some person other than himself.

Power of arrest

Any person found committing, or reasonably suspected of having committed, or having attempted to commit or being about to commit *an offence under the Act may be arrested without warrant.*

Power of search

On reasonable grounds *a justice may grant a search warrant authorising any constable named therein to enter at any time any premises or place named and to search same and every person found therein and to seize any document or thing found in connection with which there is reasonable ground for suspecting that an offence under the Act has been or is about to be committed.*

These laws and powers are horrifying if you consider their full implications. It means that any person, or group of people, who protest against injustices in the status quo can be arrested for sedition, and if they write about them they can be charged with seditious libel (regardless of the fact that what they wrote was true). It means that any time a socio-political movement threatens the status quo it can, at the whim of 'the State', become 'proscribed', making all the people involved in it terrorists and subject to all the restrictions of the Prevention of Terrorism Act. It means that regardless how scurrilous, immoral and dangerous are the acts or intentions of Government departments or individuals therein we, the people, can be forbidden from hearing about them — let alone DOING anything about them — by the simple expedient of invoking the Official Secrets Act on the spurious grounds of 'endangering National Security'. It means that anybody *reasonably suspected* of being *about to commit a crime* can be arrested without warrant and that on the *reasonable grounds* arbitrarily decided by a justice ANYBODY'S house can be broken into and searched together with all its inmates and ANY document can be seized (like this book, for instance) on the grounds that it may contain material 'prejudicial to the safety or interest of the State'. The fact that these laws are not at present upheld to the letter is because the "State" (acting solely on behalf of the self-interested elements of society most anxious to avoid any threats to their comfortable status quo) does not regard itself under imminent threat, but the moment it does (as with the striking miners) they all come to the surface like beetles from the woodwork to repress, restrict and ultimately defeat any attempt to challenge the interests of the "State". Economic recession, mass unemployment and social unrest are all that are required to expose the true, vindictive nature of our Law and Order, to spotlight its true targets and to turn the system we call democracy into a malicious and repressive Police State.

Crime is, overwhelmingly, the crime of the poor as defined by the rich. The huge crimes committed against humanity every hour of every day by the rich and powerful are not recognized within the Law and go completely unpunished. As a result of the actions of the people in control of big businesses, millions of people die every year, but this is not considered a crime. Tobacco companies sell death-dealing cigarettes to millions upon millions of people every year, but they are troubled neither by their conscience nor by the Law — and now that the people of the industrialized countries are beginning to reject them they are turning to the people of the third world — high tar and all and NO government warning. Drug companies knowingly foist useless and dangerous drugs that have been rejected by rich countries onto the unsuspecting poor. For years, concerned people have been trying to stop multi-nationals from selling expensive milk powder to poor countries and convincing trusting mothers that it is better for their babies when not only is the mother's milk infinitely superior but making up bottles in unhygienic conditions, often with contaminated water, *KILLS*. The bastards know this, but they still do it; in the name of profit, in the name of *GREED*. But they are not punished. There is no law to stop them. Every day, people die from industrial diseases and accidents because the rich have not taken the necessary measures to protect the workers. Every day thousands of people die because the rich are stockpiling the means of their survival, in the name of profit, in the name of greed. Yet they will not be punished. No law accuses THEM of stealing or killing. Nobody locks THEM up and accuses them of moral inferiority; THEY award themselves knighthoods and call their crimes 'services to industry'.

If a crime is an act committed against humanity it seems to me that society's accusing fingers are being pointed in the wrong directions, and the Law is truly an ass.

4. THE CHURCH

The centrepiece of Judeo-Christian religious imagery is a white, male God and the established Church is, and always has been, run by well-heeled, upper class, white men. It is a right-wing, patriarchal institution run in the interests, and from the viewpoint, of rich, powerful, white men. It is used as a tool by the rich to control the poor, by whites to control blacks (sorry, BLECKS) and by men to control women. Man was built in the image of God, we are told, and God is white — so if you are black, or a woman, you are automatically inferior, soul-less and subordinate and should be prepared to spend your whole life in subservience.

The Church, as we all know, vehemently refutes this unkind appraisal of it. The Church, it maintains, is A-political, just like all the rest of our established institutions; and just as with all the rest of our established institutions, if it does NOTHING to attempt to alter the status quo or to influence present day politics then it is in fact tacitly supporting the right wing. Only the other day I heard a Church man say of his involvement with CND (unusual in itself) that he didn't want people to associate him with "the trendy left", or anything. Shock horror. I suppose he thinks that if he doesn't associate himself with the left it makes him neutral — but how can anyone sit back and pretend that by doing NOTHING the world will miraculously become a better place to live in? What, I wonder, does he imagine 'neutral' politics actually means? Since we live under a right-wing system how can upholding that system (by doing nothing to change it) possibly be termed a 'neutral' attitude? What, for that matter, does he think he means by 'trendy left'? "Trendy" humanitarianism? Does the Church REALLY imagine that condemning peasants in the third world who take up arms and fight back against vicious, right-wing oppression will miraculously effect a change of heart in the oppressors and put an end to the unremitting violence at present in operation? Surely, if the Church was worth its salt as a humanitarian body it would stand up and say "Letting people die of starvation in their millions whilst others stockpile food or throw it away in the interests of profit is INTOLERABLE. Allowing people to be tortured, starved and oppressed in the interests of the pure *GREED* of others is INTOLERABLE. The system under which we conduct our affairs and under which this kind of inhumanity is allowed to continue must change, in the name of God and morality, and we must work towards instating a system that will make the world a more equitable and humane place to live in." If holy men were to preach THAT message from their pulpits on Sundays perhaps they might do some good to the world. But Church policy does nothing to condemn capitalism, even though everybody in the Church must know that it is a system that necessitates all kinds of totally unchristian behaviour, any more than it raises its voice against the greed of the rich or the totally immoral operations of corporate industry. Its message to the poor, the oppressed and the hopeless is not "rise up and together we will achieve justice" but "do nothing, don't complain and perhaps one day the meek will inherit the earth — and if not, perhaps something better will turn up when you're dead". Reading between the lines, what that really means is "Don't go causing revolutions and upsetting the status quo because we're quite comfortable as we are".

Men of the cloth are ridiculously defensive when accused of preaching male superiority, and equally ludicrously unwilling to admit that they believe God to be a man — yet the whole ethos of Christianity as taught by the Church revolves around the subordination of women to the power of men. The creation myth is a masterpiece of male invention to get round the uncomfortable reality that it is WOMEN who give birth to MEN, not vice versa; but in patriarchal Judeo-Christian imagery it was God the Father who gave birth to Adam, Adam who gave birth to Eve and God the Father who created Christ. Woman had no choice in the matter and was not an active participant in the act of creation — Mary was a mere carrier, the earth mother of spiritual man. Hence God the Father, God the Son and God the Holy Ghost were spiritually uncontaminated by the genes of woman and she was relegated to the status of bearer and caretaker of the true creator — *MAN*. Thus does man imagine that he rises above the dictates of Nature and the 'sins' of the flesh embodied in woman. Thus, supposedly, did Christ offer salvation to man — by freeing him from his shame in Eden when he was exposed to the knowledge of the pleasures of the flesh by the feeble-minded Eve. This view of women, as those responsible for man's downfall, is evident in all the Church's bigoted attitudes towards women's bodies, in its subordination of women in the Church hierarchy and in its obsessional association of 'sin' and 'morality' with the perfectly normal, human act of love-making. It is a wonder that women can hold up their heads at all under the weight of all that sin, all that guilt about defiling and contaminating otherwise pure and saintly men with their vile bodies. Man, supposedly, can find salvation in monastic asceticism away from women, but woman must be forever chained to guilt and immanence for her sins, taunted by the vision of the virgin mother as evidence of her imperfection. Redemption, methinks, should be made of sterner stuff than mere celibacy and should better be concerned with the true original sin — that of the murder of Abel by his brother Cain. Sin, it seems to me, is not rooted in the KNOWLEDGE but in the ACT — acts like rape, homicide, genocide and misanthropic cruelty — and taking the SIN out of sex exposes the true source of original sin, the true reason for the locked gates of paradise and the true path to salvation.

In the same way that it is more comfortable for men of the cloth to interpret 'sin' as having originated with woman than to admit to the culpability of their own gender, it is a good deal less painful for the rich to concentrate upon sexual activity as a yardstick of moral behaviour than it would be to start questioning the moral significance of their inordinate wealth or the price in human suffering of its preservation. Seven hundred and fifty million affluent Christians, by doing nothing at all to alter the status quo, quite happily allow one hundred and ninety-five million fellow Christians throughout the world to live in abject poverty. Is this Christian? Is this *MORAL*? Just this morning I listened with growing disgust to an account of a peasant in Chile (you know, the place where America assisted Pinochet to depose Allende's peoples' Government and the rest of the 'Christian' world stood by and watched) being pounced upon by a group of Pinochet's goons during a human rights uprising. The man was beaten, kicked and had his hair and half the top of his head hacked off, after which he was turned upside down and bounced on the top of his blood-soaked head. The reporter laconically suggested the man might never fully recover from the experience. Should not Christian men and women the world over be outraged by such atrocities? Is it moral for the Church to A-politically say NOTHING to condemn such actions and is it *MORAL* for Christians in the rich world to continue to make profits out of investments in such blood-soaked regimes? Can a church that condones such activities, or the members thereof who profit from them, ever be anything but spiritually bankrupt? Who was it who was once quoted as saying "It is easier for a camel to go through the eye of a needle than for a rich man to enter into the kingdom of God?" Seemingly the Christian church, with all its worldly wealth, has little time for such burblings — any more than its moral and righteous members.

In an equal, caring society based on the humanitarian principles that Jesus endorsed in much of his teaching there will be no worship of white, male Gods and no place for a Church that supports capitalist greed, women's subordination and the rule of the rich.

SECTION FOUR

EVERYDAY CORNBALL POLITICS

When cornballs complain that "You bring politics into everything" what it really means is that you are constantly, annoyingly, questioning what they consider is beyond question — i.e. the status quo. "Politics", says the dictionary, is:—

The science of, or a treatise on, state organisation

and since in this context we, Joe and Joanna public are, in reality, "the State" (or in governmental terms, WE are the recipients of authoritarian "State" policies), then politics represent an integral part of our everyday lives and affect everything we do — and are not something that can be turned off at will as the upholders of the status quo would have us believe. Politics not only affect external things like how our children are educated, whether or not we have nuclear power or whether or not we come out of the Common Market, they also affect our health, how we relate to one another as men and women and even how we talk to one another; and the manipulation, indoctrination and personality fragmentation that is necessary to keep the rich in power is not only damaging to health and relationships on a personal level, it threatens our very survival as a species.

1. UNHEALTHY POLITICS

Health is a manifestation of the ability of individuals to cope with internal and environmental conditions. The health of a population depends to a large degree upon how far the social system allows for individuals to be self-reliant, autonomous and dignified human beings. Health levels rise when people feel in control of their lives and confident in their ability to cope — and fall when they become dependent for their health and survival on outside influences beyond their control. Health is a natural state of happy people; sickness is an unnatural state caused by internal and external discord.

Ivan Illich, Limits to Medicine.

Our society is filled with unhealthy people who are unable to cope with internal and environmental conditions, because our social system does not allow for individuals to be self-reliant, autonomous and dignified human beings. We are, in the main, totally dependent upon outside forces for our health and survival — on being employed to earn money, or on the government if unemployed, and on being diagnosed and administered to by institutionalised medical practitioners if we get sick. The power of individuals to heal themselves by shaping their environment to make themselves happy and healthy has been expropriated by professionals and government — all of whom believe they control the secrets of health. Our lives are dictated and controlled from the time we first draw breath, and we seldom feel we have any control at all over the forces which shape our lives. Many people have given up trying to influence anything that happens to them and just shrug off world injustice and personal unhappiness in the belief that "there's nothing we can do about it so it's best to try and forget it". To earn money we often have to take the risk of exposing ourselves to dangerous materials, to work in unhealthy atmospheres with unacceptable noise levels and with people who upset us, to live in unhealthy cities full of dirt and fumes and to accept work we don't like, gives us no satisfaction and often bores us to tears. We have to put up with bosses who are arrogant, insensitive and rude and when we are humiliated and derided we have to bite our tongues and swallow our pride — to keep our jobs. Our competitive, lonely and unequal lives make us drink, smoke and take pills to try to make us happy. We eat sweets and cakes to cheer us up and end up with diabetes. To fit eating in with our hectic life styles and frantic attempts to get up there with the Trippington-Smythes we eat pre-packed food laced with chemicals and lacking in roughage and vitamins and contract cancers of the stomach and colon. We smoke cigarettes and drink alcohol to brighten our cheerless lives and get cancers and cirrhosis. Business men get heart disease and drop down dead from coronaries at earlier and earlier ages from trying to cope with the stress of unremitting competition and the constant, overhanging threat of redundancy.

So when we've been worn down by our dull lives and boring or stressful jobs and when we're sick and tired of trying to cope with all the pressures of life, that is where the whole process of professionalised health care goes into action, and there is the Doctor with his tranquillizers and his long words, his high technology solutions and his spare parts. The numbers of physical and mental disorders with fancy names that Doctors come up with are staggering, and each one has a pill or a psychological theory to put it right. Health has become incredibly complicated and, considering how much modern medicine now revolves around complicated machinery and expensive drugs, *very* pricey. Our ill health has become very big business and an awful lot of people would be very upset by an outbreak of good health.

There is a glaringly obvious solution to the sickness in our society, which is to alter the system under which we live to enable the people to be happy — and hence to be healthy. It is so glaringly obvious that anybody who really thinks about it for a moment should be asking themselves "why has nobody in the medical profession SUGGESTED it?". Why are millions of pounds and the lives of thousands of animals still being squandered on research into wonder drugs to combat cancer when we all KNOW what causes the majority of cancers? Why is all the emphasis in medicine placed on 'treating the symptoms' rather than on 'eliminating the causes'? Why, when everybody is having to suffer the cuts in the health service by losing hospitals and staff and having to do without basic amenities is there still an annual drugs bill of £2,000 millions and rising, and why, when the health service is supposed to be bankrupt, is the emphasis still on treating the minority with high technology equipment and 'brand new cures' (most of which turn out to be useless) instead of stretching the resources and giving primary health care to the MAJORITY? Why is there still such a fascination with powerful drugs, when it has been proved that they cause more sickness than they cure by masking the underlying causes of disease, by setting up allergies and adverse and secondary reactions and by destroying the body's defence mechanisms? Why has there been no pressure from the medical profession on the government to create the conditions necessary to stop their patients getting sick? Why do Doctors continue to close their eyes to underlying social causes of disease and mental disorders and dish out pills? Why do they not protest, repeatedly, noisily and vociferously, when they KNOW that all they are doing is patching up the results of a degenerate, pathogenic society? They are not difficult questions to answer when you realise one important factor — that the controlling body of medicine is dominated by those same rich, white men that are at the root of all our problems, and that Doctors are trained in medical schools whose controlling bodies are dominated by rich, white men, all of whose priorities are identical — the maintenance and defence of the existing capitalist status quo. It then becomes apparent why medicine is so wedded to expensive drugs, expensive cures and high technology, because they provide a means of making a PROFIT. It then becomes obvious that drugs are a useful tool in keeping the people quiet about their unhappiness and ill health and in preventing them from searching for the real causes. The obsession for cure-alls and wonder drugs — so that we can all continue to be filled up like dustbins with consumer items and escapist drugs, live in fume-ridden cities and work in unhealthy and stressful conditions and take a PILL to get rid of the cancers and disease it all results in — becomes eminently understandable. Take the pill, have the operation, make use of the wondrous equipment — but don't THINK, don't DELVE, don't make uncomfortable connections of cause and effect. A wonder drug indeed — but for who? A wonder drug to keep us quiet, keep us working, keep us accepting the unacceptable; keep taking the pill and keep safeguarding their profits. That way they have to do NOTHING to alter the status quo.

Of course we, the public, DO have an option. We can refuse to buy consumer rubbish, refuse to take their valium and barbiturates, refuse to kill ourselves making huge profits for tobacco companies — and at the same time DEMAND that the system is radically altered to improve the quality of our lives so that we do not have to do boring, stressful and unrewarding work and live unequal, unhappy and unhealthy lives. A novel idea.

'Consider two thousand years trying to reconcile a philanthropic mentor with a misanthropic social system. What has that done to the human Psyche? What has it made of human society?'

2. POLITICS, GENDER AND MORALITY

The psychology involved in keeping upper class Henry in power, unchallenged, generation after generation, is not only an insidious means of manipulation, it is also an extremely dangerous and destructive phenomenon because it is largely unrecognised — even by those who are supposedly in control of it — as a mere psychological con-trick, and what were originally a series of convenient myths concocted to keep women and other men in their power have now become a trap to ensnare the very instigators of the deception. The lies have been repeated so often, so loudly and in so many different ways that even the liars themselves now believe them — but make no mistake, they *ARE* lies, it *IS* illusion, it *IS* a deception. I am talking, of course, about the moral superiority of the upper class and about their God-given rights to privilege and at the same time, and in the same breath, I am talking about the moral and spiritual inferiority of women.

The myth of upper class superiority is not built solely around money, it is also built around an assumed set of characteristics, which in themselves are connected to differences of gender in the following manner:—

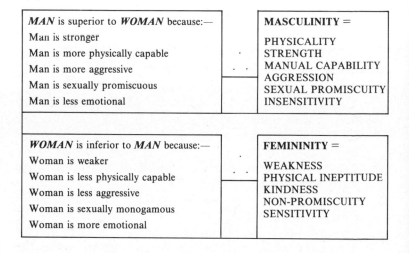

MAN is superior to *WOMAN* because:—		MASCULINITY =
Man is stronger		PHYSICALITY
Man is more physically capable	·	STRENGTH
Man is more aggressive	· ·	MANUAL CAPABILITY
Man is sexually promiscuous		AGGRESSION
Man is less emotional		SEXUAL PROMISCUITY
		INSENSITIVITY

WOMAN is inferior to *MAN* because:—		FEMININITY =
Woman is weaker	·	WEAKNESS
Woman is less physically capable	· ·	PHYSICAL INEPTITUDE
Woman is less aggressive		KINDNESS
Woman is sexually monogamous		NON-PROMISCUITY
Woman is more emotional		SENSITIVITY

This set of assumed characteristics forms the whole basis of man's supposed superiority over women and the means by which he holds on to his power. But how does he hold on to his power over the lower orders and convince them of his moral superiority over them? It presents a bit of a problem, given the following social equation of morality.

GOD (GOODNESS) INTELLECTUAL SEXUALLY PURE SENSITIVE REFINED (CIVILISED)	**NATURE (EVIL)** PHYSICAL PROMISCUOUS BRUTAL ANIMALISTIC (UNCIVILISED)

Now, a cursory examination of these two sets of equations will show that the characteristics associated with nature and evil are far closer to the characteristics associated with masculinity than to those of femininity. With this in mind, how does upper class man hold on to his (contrived) masculine characteristics denoting his superiority over women, yet at the same time assume God-like qualities to convince the lower orders of their inferiority? Well the answer is that he can't, and the compromises he makes constitute a disaster in all our lives.

To begin at the beginning of this sorry tale it will be necessary to explain, for the benefit of all those who do not know, what it is that the upper class believe about themselves and how they justify their privileged position and inordinate wealth both to themselves and (they hope) to the rest of us.

1. *The rich are rich because they are superior beings.*
2. *The rich have different values to the poor and do not live by base instinct alone.*
3. *The upper class are intelligent beings born to be rulers and administrators.*
4. *The poor are unintelligent, physical beings born to do menial work and obey THEM.*
5. *The rich are more virtuous than the poor and therefore closer to God.*
6. *God, via their representatives in the Church, accepts* <u>*inherited*</u> *wealth but doesn't approve of Mammon (i.e. the dirty business of acquiring it if you weren't born with it).*

With the help of school, the Church and the rest of the establishment upper class man can get across many of these messages quite successfully and the unholy rat race going on below him to acquire the few crumbs he knocks off his abundant (inherited) table is a definite advantage in making him appear morally superior, as he rises above it in saintly fashion and allows all those below him to take the rap for his dirty work. But it is not enough, and in order to make the illusion of superiority STICK, both in his own mind and in the minds of those below him, his whole life has to become an obvious and noticeable distinction between HIM and THEM (the lower orders) and between THEM (men) and US (women) and revolves around this third equation — the class equation in relation to women.

POWER

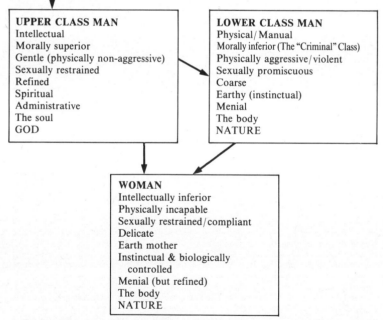

UPPER CLASS MAN
Intellectual
Morally superior
Gentle (physically non-aggressive)
Sexually restrained
Refined
Spiritual
Administrative
The soul
GOD

LOWER CLASS MAN
Physical/Manual
Morally inferior (The "Criminal" Class)
Physically aggressive/violent
Sexually promiscuous
Coarse
Earthy (instinctual)
Menial
The body
NATURE

WOMAN
Intellectually inferior
Physically incapable
Sexually restrained/compliant
Delicate
Earth mother
Instinctual & biologically
   controlled
Menial (but refined)
The body
NATURE

In order to keep alive the myths surrounding their assumed airs of superiority, the upper class have strict codes of behaviour and woebetide any black(?) sheep that strays from them and betrays the class. Their greatest fear is of discovery, of being found out in their dishonesty and laid bare in all their insecurity, vulnerability and moral imperfection — and the greatest crime they can commit against their class is indiscretion. For this reason they keep very much to themselves, in case the lower orders become familiar and start to see them for what they are — a load of upper class bores and parasites — in place of how they want to be seen — a superior race with different values and a higher morality. Their appearance is of tantamount importance and must always give an impression of refined gentility, both at work and at play. Henry at work must be pin-striped, immaculately creased and impeccably polished at all times. He must not display any such animal tendencies as facial hair or dirty finger nails, the hair on his head must be neat and respectably short and he must NEVER wear anything flamboyant, expressive or over-colourful, or anything likely to be suggestive of his sexuality like — saints preserve us — a pair of TIGHT trousers. At play Henries and Henriettas, (along with striving upper-middles and right-wing intellectuals) can be seen enjoying such refined pastimes as classical opera, ballet, music and theatre, suitably attired in their suitably refined apparel with modest shows of oyster diseases clipped on to dead seals as a mark of worth. The upper classes have traditionally held a virtual monopoly of 'The Arts' (which means, overwhelmingly, the classical arts) and have largely excluded the masses through a combination of expense, the intimidating requirements of dress and behaviour and a kind of tacit understanding that they alone are capable of appreciating such civilised artistic outlets.[1] They alone, they believe, have a definitive

1. *Whereas it is undoubtedly true that most of us in the lower orders don't enjoy classical literature, art and entertainment in the same way as those who have undergone many years of sophisticated, elitist education, it is debatable that this validates 'The Classics' being used as the criterion against which all other forms should be judged, whether they should continue to form the whole basis for artistic studies and whether they should be subsidised so heavily to the detriment of community art projects, 'fringe' theatre and contemporary dance and music. After all, is the asexual refinement of classical ballet **REALLY** any more aesthetic and poignant than **West Side Story**, is **Tommy** less valid than **Carmen**, or 'The Female Eunuch' and 'The Ragged Trousered Philanthropists' any less worthy of serious and analytical study than 'Kim' or 'The Mayor of Casterbridge'? Or are the favoured choices just more 'traditional' and hence more politically acceptable? Surely if full appreciation of the classics depends upon so much intensive education and if this education can realistically only be given to a minority of the population, then such elitist pursuits should be regarded as 'fringe' with a 'fringe' budget, and not as mainstream with colossal funding? It must be within the bounds of possibility that the majority of us actually **PREFER** post 1940's 'rock' culture and have no desire to 'understand' — much less revert to — traditional upper class pursuits and straight-laced cornball culture.*

understanding of the meaning of 'art', and the soul resides exclusively in the bosoms of the initiated. At work as at home, no Henry worth his silver spoon would be caught doing anything physical, like changing a plug or digging the estate, and WORK invariably means juggling with finances, prodding figures into computers and shuffling papers around desks — always intellectual, never manual, always administrative, never participatory (useful), always important, never menial. Henry is the mind, not the body.

Henry's refined manner and physical weakness would make it difficult for him to maintain his assumed air of masculine superiority over woman if she were allowed to remain her normal self, so she has been moulded to complement his image of himself as the 'gentle'-man. In order that he may still appear masculine, strong, physically capable and sexually dominant, woman has had to become ultra-feminine, ultra-weak, ultra-incapable and sexually dependent upon his lead. Her body has had to become ultra-smooth to contrast with what is left of his secondary sexual characteristics after he has finished trying to disguise them in a self-conscious veil of refinement and she has been condemned as 'emotionaly unstable and intellectually feeble' so that he may appear a rock of masculine reliability and intellectual superiority.

In everyday life, sexual stereotyping and the use of assumed sexual characteristics to divide human beings into superior and inferior, moral and immoral categories has largely undesirable effects. The working class stereotype male — cornball physical Pete — is uncouth, insensitive, sexually inhibited (being unable to relate to women) and often physically violent. He hates homosexuals and effeminate men (which is why, as much as anything else, Henry keeps out of his way), and has no interest in any of Henry's supposedly ultra-civilised pastimes. Pete is a pub and football man and all his thoughts are macho, physical, aggressive and decidedly unrefined. His work is usually physically demanding, menial, usually boring and invariably intellectually unstimulating. Cornball Pete is physicality personified.

Middle class Oliver dresses himself in suits and ties and mimics the upper class in an attempt to absorb their social status. However badly paid and badly treated by those above him, Oliver's allegiance lies unswervingly to management and the rich. Striving Olivers are full of pretention, confusion and schizophrenia and don't know if they're on their arses or their elbows. Their fear of contravening Henry's rules of social decorum and betraying their social origins leaves them friendless, opinionless and scared shitless in case they use the wrong knife or the wrong expression, wear the wrong clothes or buy the wrong settee, eat the wrong food or get caught fraternising with the wrong people, drink the wrong wine at the wrong temperature or wipe their arses on an unfashionable bog-roll. Their choice of entertainment and leisure activities leave them in a constant quandary between the pretention of the opera, the thuggery of football and the expense of the golf club. Quite often it all gets too much and they stay at home and watch the television (should I REALLY admit I watch Coronation Street to the wags at the office?) or dig the garden — but not too strenuously. When the struggle about Gnomes and mock Georgian pillars gets too much in the garden they toddle off down to the saloon bar of the local and sip ale out of a straight pint glass with the local conservatives, exchange a few risqué jokes and one or two daring remarks about coons and toddle back home again. Their fear of being associated with the working class leaves their sexuality submerged in loose fitting, shapeless apparel and Victorian puritanism, while their intellect is allowed little or no expression in their mundane employment. The upper class don't accept them, the blue collar workers despise them for their uselessness and they are in constant competition with their own kind, both at work and at home. All-in-all a truly unenviable bunch. No wonder so many of them end up on shrink couches searching for their identity — I certainly wouldn't want to be the one trying to find it.

Cornball Henry is equally restricted in his daily activities since he is confined to such small, claustrophobic circles — and quite apart from his sexless appearance he is devoid of attractiveness in any other direction. He is excruciatingly boring because there are so many topics he dare not broach and so many aspects of life about which he lives in

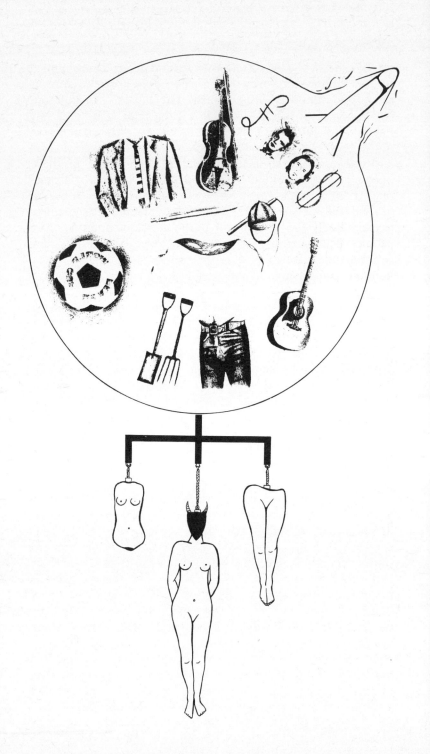

total ignorance. His social conversation tends to be limited to one-upmanship over the plebs and social climbers, school, hunting, shooting, opera and horses. His humour, being confined to his worldly experiences, is limited and puerile. He has never mixed in the real world, so he knows nothing of real-world humour. Much humour springs from hardship and the struggles of life, and as Henry has never known any except in his childhood when he was constantly bullied at school, his sense of humour never develops beyond the classroom. He thinks any small joke he makes is exceedingly funny and will repeat it many times to many people, bellowing like a bull each time, or snuffling and snorting uncontrollably. He likes dirty, schoolboy (lavatory) humour and sniggers delightedly and lecherously at any mention of tits and bums and s . . . e . . . x. His sheltered, segregated upbringing leaves him totally bemused about the opposite s . . . e . . . x except that they are his inferiors and he may be expected to marry one of them one day for the sake of respectability. His entertainment, when he's not at the opera or the ballet or out killing something in the country in an attempt to salvage some of his lost manhood at the expense of some poor wretched animal, is severely limited by the fact that he cannot be involved in anything suggestive of sex or associated with the lower orders. All black music is prohibited by the upperclass association of blacks with the jungle, which rules out R & B, Blues, Negro Spirituals and Jazz. Nothing in the heavy rock area can be considered, and refined noses twitch in disapproval at the blatant displays of sexuality in tight trousers, delicate features blush and turn aside from such openly suggestive gestures. Just about anything that came from the sixties is unthinkable, rife as it all is with permissive lyrics and subversive notions. Folk music is out because most of the singers have too much facial hair and sing about the imagined grievances of the peasants. Not much is left but the safe, traditional old classics, and that's where Henry usually ends up. As for dancing — well, anyone who has ever watched a Henry gyrating in opposition to a piece of music will KNOW how little he believes his body belongs to him and how much he fervently wishes it would go away and leave him alone. Dancing is just too, too *physical*.

Female stereotypes lose out all ways because they not only have to conform to the rigid, stereotyped characteristics which supposedly constitute 'femininity', they also have to conform to their partners' class rules — the lamentable result of which is sexless, brainless, physically incapable travesties of what started out as human beings, dancing to the tune of patriarchal dominance and class snobbery like frilly, pink puppets on a silver string; the punch-bags of male insecurity, the dustbins for male sin and male guilt and the criterion for masculine superiority. The stereotype woman has become everything that man does not want to be — his externalised, personified disgust with himself. She is his weakness, his sexual desire, his emotional need, his compassion, his dependence and his fragility. She is mother nature, sin, the flesh and a reminder of his animal origins. She, uncomplainingly, must suffer so that he, in a pure and Godlike state, can triumph. She, the puppet queen of contrived femininity, is a constant reminder of his imperfection — an ever present, ever despised obstacle to his salvation. Without her he can beget without sin, without her he can live in eternal purity with his heavenly father . . .

Somewhere, in amongst these rigid, suffocating stereotypes are real human beings crying out for recognition. In between the brute physicality of Pete and the pious, intellectual refinement of Henry lie a body and a mind longing to be re-united. Somewhere between the pure, intellectual Henry who can't change a plug and whose body has atrophied through lack of use, and the coarse, physical Pete whose brain has atrophied and whose sensitivity has been steam-rollered, lies a sensitive, intelligent person with a fully capable body. Somewhere between Pete's obsessive preoccupation with sexual conquest and Henry's obsessive preoccupation with restraint lies the capacity for healthy, sexual enjoyment. Somewhere between Henry's disguise, and Pete's over-emphasis, of sexual characteristics lies a genuine sexual identity.

Somewhere underneath it all is a male and a female. Somewhere between the sharing, caring, all-emotional female and the brutal, warmongering, all-insensitive male are two worried, disjointed people. Somewhere between the physically incapable, dependent woman with no intellect who must stay in the home and bring up children and the ultra-capable male who must go out to work and become totally financially responsible for his dependents are two people who would enjoy looking after children, enjoy spending some time IN the home and some time OUT of it, who would both enjoy times of being supported and times of responsibility, who would both like to be physically capable, mentally in control of their everyday activities and free from dependence on anybody else for their survival.

Somewhere behind the façade of this dreadful masquerade can be found the same basic human needs — the desire for sexual gratification, the need for physical and mental stimulation, the need to be in control of events and the need to exchange emotions with other humans. These needs exist regardless of gender, regardless of colour and regardless of artificially created notions of "class", and stereotyping men and women and assigning them characteristics according to their stereotyped gender/class/ group image is damaging and dangerous. Henry, Pete, Oliver and the stereotype woman are not natural human beings — they are all just *PARTS* of human beings, each living fragmented existences with one or two of the characteristics of human totality exaggerated out of all proportion. This leads not only to unhappy, confused people with stunted minds and repressed, distorted sexuality, it also has dangerous side effects. Henry, due to his obsession with God and purity and his own narcissistic vision of himself as a superior being becomes, if not sexually incapable, severely sexually repressed in his mind. He cannot allow himself to enjoy sex, since sex (the 'physical') is associated with the beast and the lower orders, and woman is associated in his mind with the earth, nature and the flesh. He sees himself as the essence of purity, the essence of intellectuality. The homosexual taboo means that if he takes that route to avoiding contact with the evil influence of woman and indulging his narcissistic male arrogance, he could get himself in trouble socially unless he's very careful; so he has to find a substitute for sex. He laments the loss of his masculinity (as defined by man to control woman) and since that masculinity represents power he has to find another means of controlling other men, another visible means of demonstrating his power. So he builds himself huge, external symbols and imagines that these, and the national power they represent, will take the place of his personal loss. He thinks he can submerge himself in power and ignore the torment that is going on inside him but he can't, and in place of the phallic symbols he created they become ever-present reminders of his personal emasculation, taunting him with his own mortality, his vulnerability, his needs and his origins. All his money and all his power cannot transform him into the God he longs to be and his fury knows no bounds; so he turns his frustration and anger against all the things that he believes to represent his own weakness. He hates the earth, mother earth, symbol of Nature, symbol of his arrogant, Godlike war against his own sexual yearning and human needs. He wants to pierce her with his weapons, destroy her, bombard her in a frenzied rage against her for making him imperfect. In his darkest, most irrational thoughts, woman is the sole reason for his downfall and if he can destroy her he will be saved. Nuclear weapons are his ultimate lunacy, his last ditch attempt to become one with God by destroying the earth, symbol of Nature, symbol of woman, symbol of imperfection.

But Henry cannot destroy the earth without destroying himself, and it is high time he was made to acknowledge that fact. Henry's idea of perfection is absurd and has nothing whatever to do with being human. Human beings fuck to procreate — they don't arrive by immaculate conception — so Henry (and the rest of humanity with him) should learn to accept that fundamental reality of human existence and ENJOY it, instead of feeling ashamed about it and trying to repress it. God and Nature cannot be two separate entities because humans beings are DEPENDENT upon the forces of Nature for their survival and if we destroy, or try to defeat, Nature, then we destroy and defeat ourselves. Man and woman cannot be two separate species, one good, one bad, one important, one subordinate, one God, one servant — because they DEPEND upon one another for their survival. Henry, in order to save himself and the rest of us with him must be made to confront these realities and to admit that only by re-uniting God and Nature can his mind be re-united with his body, can woman regain her dignity as an equal being and can we all regain our souls. If man ceases to view compassion as being synonymous with weakness, then he can afford to be compassionate. If sexuality is not synonymous with bestiality and inferiority, Henry can afford to express his sexuality and can afford to allow Pete the dignity of regaining his intellect. If woman is not synonymous with sin he can allow her to be recognised as an equal being, with equal sexual desires, equal intellect and equal rights to pursue her own happiness. If Nature is not synonymous with evil, he can afford to let the earth survive and put away his terrible phallic weapons in favour of a good fuck.

If we are ever to heal and reconcile the damaging social and personality divisions that permeate and sour our whole society, and if we are to be spared the lunacy of a nuclear winter, then Henry's power, his superiority, his twisted morality and his opinion of women must all be seriously challenged — and radically altered. If the ailing human psyche is ever to find peace then the philanthropy in the human conscience must be reflected in human behaviour, and in the social system that moulds it. Only then will Christian morality be reconciled with the politics of our everyday lives.

3. TALKING POLITICS

Cornballs quickly become agitated, exasperated, irritated and eventually, if not immediately, downright nasty if you ask them to explain what they mean when they use well-known and well-established words and expressions to emphasize a point they are labouring to make — because cornballs do not feel they have any obligation, social or moral, to explain anything to anybody in connection with what they do and say. They therefore feel perfectly justified in using such empty and mindless expressions as:

"Oh isn't he adorable. He's a real little BOY"

and expect everybody else to draw their own conclusions as to what the bloody hell it actually MEANS. Likewise with:—

"It's a man's world, but women are the ones who get what they want".

"The rich are alright, but I can't STAND the nouveau riche. Pretentious upstarts".

"Socialism is alright in theory but it wouldn't work in practice".

"It's a free country".

"He's so effeminate".

"Men never grow up".

"He's a man of the world".

"I like a man to BE a man . . . and a woman to be a woman".

"They are SO well bred".

"He's such an animal".

"Don't be such a bloody woman".

"That's not a NORMAL way to behave".

Haven't we all heard those, ad nauseam? Of course — they are everyday, commonplace expressions. But if you look at them clinically they are absolutely meaningless remarks — unless you are prepared to endow them with the hidden messages and weighted associations that they are all intended to convey. Each one of those expressions — and the hundreds like them — is a means of exchanging, in a few words, the shared indoctrination of a lifetime. Women and animals are inferior; men and women are opposites; Superiority is inherited; 'normal' (i.e. sane, correct, acceptable) is 'the way things are'; Socialists are dreamers, capitalists are realists . . . and so on. None of this is A-political, as the cornball would have us believe. All those assumptions are rooted in a patriarchal, aristocratic/plutocratic power base and each expression enforces the prejudices that form the basis of the present status quo.

Such political bias is not just an everyday part of cornball speech, it is actively fanned and fostered in the language used constantly by the right wing establishment. For example, "PROPAGANDA", in terms of dictionary definition, means:—

"Association or scheme for propagating a doctrine or practice", but the way it is used lends it a much more complex and sinister meaning. It is invariably associated with the imagined devious practices of 'the left' and is tacitly connected to communism, dictatorship and loss of freedom, and if the right-wing press wants to discredit any effort to improve or abolish any oppressive, right-wing practice, it insinuates the word 'Propaganda' into the article and leaves the already well-established implications of the word to worm its way into the consciousness of the readers and poison them against the proposition. Fanatic is a word never used to describe people like Margaret Thatcher or the present Tory ministers (Fowler, for example), but is overworked on people like Tony Benn and Arthur Scargill — as though it is automatically 'left' to be fanatical (i.e. wrong, not *RIGHT* and correct). Women who complain about their treatment by the patriarchs or try to change any of society's myriad injustices are branded 'strident' (loud, discordant) and those who dare, in any way, to try to determine their own destiny or assert their identity are 'unnatural', 'career women', 'unfeminine' — or all three. The word 'anarchy' is used by the right-wing media to indicate a state of disorganisation and chaos caused by a lack of control and an absence of authority — yet anybody who has bothered to find out what Anarchists believe will know that organisation is the very essence of their philosophy. The fact that ordinary people, i.e. all those not in CONTROL, are considered incapable of taking responsibility for themselves and are not deemed capable of organisation without authority is yet another indication of the arrogance of those in power who, by implication, deem themselves BETTER than the rest of us, because WE need THEM to show us how to live. It implies that without their AUTHORITY we would not have the wonderful, peaceful, well-organised and blissfully happy community we enjoy at present and that Anarchists are bent upon upsetting the wondrous harmony that our morally and intellectually superior rulers have bestowed upon us in their infinite wisdom. It's a real wonder how it is that we manage to organise our domestic lives without one of THEM in the cupboard. (Although perhaps I shouldn't tempt fate.)

A casual glance at the following associations listed in Roget's Thesaurus provides a fairly good illustration of the cultural bias inherent in the language and the number of assumptions that slip through unquestioned (all emphasis myown).

ANIMAL: *Inferior, mindless, unthinking, intemperate.*

AGGRESSIVE: *Vigorous, violent, active, quarrelling, attacking, contending, warlike, courageous.*

ARISTOCRACY: *Superiority, nation, Government.*

ARISTOCRAT: *Proud MAN, nob, swell, GENT, superior person.*

ARISTOCRATIC: *Governmental, worshipful, genteel.*

ART CRITIC: *Spectator, MAN of taste.*

BARBARIAN: *Foreigner, destroyer, vulgar, low fellow, PLEBEIAN.*

BARON: *NOBLEman, Judge.*

BEGGAR: *Wanderer, idler, recipient, poor man, LOW FELLOW.*

BEGGARLY: *Dirty, beggarly, disreputable, not nice, vulgar, PLEBEIAN, DISHONEST.*

BOURGEOISIE: *Mediocrity, commonality.*

BRUTE CREATION: *Animality, non-intellect.*

BRUTISH: *Plebeian, discourteous, cruel, sensual.*

CAD: *Non-conformist, vulgarian, low fellow, hateful object.*

CAPITALISM: *Barter, equivalence, interchange, trade, swop.*

CAPITALIST: *Director, master, moneyer, rich man.*

CASTRATE: *Subtract, unman, sterilize, make useless, impair.*

CATASTROPHE: *REVOLUTION!*

CELEBRITY: *Made MAN, famousness.*

CHAIR*MAN*: *Superior, director, master.*

IMPOTENT: *Unimportant, non-active, pitiful, pitiable, weak, pathetic, powerless, inferior.*

IMPURITY: *Uncleanliness, bad-taste, libido, wickedness, sensualism, indelicacy, coarseness, sex, dirt, filth, obscenity.*

NOBLE:	*Important, well-bred, proud, honourable, pedigreed, Royal, well-born, grand.*
NOBILITY:	*Superiority, elite, beauty, aristocracy, disinterestedness, humility, no thought for self, self-denial.*
POTENCY:	*Power, strength, utility.*
POWERFUL:	*Potent, multi-potent, mighty, great, influential, almighty, rich, OMNIPOTENT, competent, capable, able, effectual, effective, successful, BELLICOSE, warlike, with resources.*
PURE:	*Perfect, undefiled, sinless, virginal, maidenly, unwedded, impregnable, uncorruptible, frigid, cold, spotless, snowy, white, good, honourable, moral, virtuous.* *MORAL:— Pure, PIOUS, good, kind, decent, respectful, faithful, spiritual, saintly, Christian, full of grace.*
SEDITIOUS:	*Revolutionary, DISOBEDIENT.*
UNMAN:	*Palsy, cowardise, DEVITALIZE, weaken, emasculate, castrate, caponize, EFFEMINATE.*
VITALITY:	*Healthiness, health, vigour, liveliness, virility, red-bloodedness, manliness, male, resolution, AGGRESSIVENESS, BELLICOSITY, physique, muscularity, Titanic strength.*

The number of assumptions in those few words is staggering. It is quite obviously and inarguably written from the point of view of an upper class, white man who undoubtedly believes that the aristocracy is comprised entirely of men and that those men are the superior, natural-born rulers of humanity. He is obsessed by the evil of sex and sees morality in terms of piety, virginity and frigidity. To be a 'good' person, it seems, entails being "frigid and virginal (if a woman), snowy-white and Christian", and his description of "impurity" certainly leaves nobody in any doubt about his convictions. To be poor and beggarly is to be dishonest, disreputable and not nice, whereas to be rich and noble is to be honourable, proud and grand. To be a member of the nobility is to be superior and elite, and generally to be associated with beauty and morality (even, he seems to believe, with self-denial, humility and "with no thought for self" — but perhaps that was a misprint). His idea of capitalism as mere barter and fair exchange naively ignores such basic and fundamental associations as exploitation, profit and greed and his description of capitalists is definitely that of a 'gentleman' rather than a worker, who might enlarge a bit on the associations. It is interesting to note in passing how he distastefully associates the bourgeoisie with 'commonality and mediocrity', and should be an eye-opener to those of the middle classes who like to ally themselves with the superiority of the 'uppers'. He finally blows his cool completely, and blatantly describes revolution as a catastrophe.

Of course it could be argued that since Roget wrote Thesaurus in the mid 19th century the ideas and associations expressed in it should be regarded as those of Victorian England, not of the 1980's — and I wholeheartedly agree. But then if that is the case, why are they still being expressed by my copy of the book, which was printed in 1978 and is supposed to represent an up-to-date reflection of present day attitudes and provide an up-to-date reference for crossword punters and the like? Why, in 1978, is it still assumed that art critics are automatically and exclusively male, why has chair*MAN* not become chair*PERSON* and why is there no wider description of 'feminist' beyond that of 'female'? Why is no mention made of the women's movement and why, under 'women and children' do we merely see 'encumbrance'? Do we (or do those who are supposed to do the revising and updating) really believe that the Royals and the upper class are fed on royal jelly to make them different — or are they just fed on public money and resources? Are the members of the upper class REALLY the superior breed they would have us believe they are? Since the answers are, unquestionably, no they are NOT a superior breed and yes the ARE just a load of parasites living off the backs of the rest of the community, then what is the excuse for Thesaurus still to be describing the upper and lower classes in the following terms — unless the updaters are trying to keep alive delusions of upper class grandeur and moral superiority? (all emphasis my own).

UPPER CLASSES	LOWER CLASSES
Top layer, first families, best people, better sort, chosen few, elite, ruling class, <u>the twice born</u>, authority, high ups, OLYMPIANS	*Lower orders, ONE'S INFERIORS, inferior, common sort, small fry, lesser breed, great unwashed, working class, second class citizens, outcasts, beatniks, beat generation, underworld, low company, low life, dunghill, slum*

Not a very pretty picture of what the poor old working classes are supposedly about, is it? Nor is the picture any prettier for women, or for humanity's chances of survival, if you analyse some of the assumptions that are being made by the use of such words as 'aggressive, castrate, impotent, powerful, unman and vitality'. The dictionary definition of 'aggressive' is "To perpetrate an unprovoked attack", but the associations of the word as listed in Thesaurus are the spurious and dangerous associations of a capitalistic, patriarchal society. By implication, any man who considers himself 'non-aggressive' in the sense that he is a pacifist must at the same time leave himself open to the criticism that he is 'non-energetic, non-manly, non-competitive and (again by association) unsuccessful'. A non-aggressive man is therefore considered a failure by our society. The associations are indeed spurious, but are used to great advantage by those who wish to harness the nation's energy for their own ends. Any woman who repeatedly asserts her opinions in her job is open to the criticism of being aggressive, which when applied to a woman is intended as an insult, since for a woman to be 'manly, warlike, violent and contentious' is as much a crime as for a man to be 'effeminate, passive and compassionate'. A woman, therefore, cannot be *energetic* without being aggressive, and neither men nor women can be either without being competitive. From there, it is a short step to the assumption that 'women were meant to stay in the home, be inactive in the outside world and not display an abundance of (aggressive) energy', and that men were 'meant' to be warlike and competitive in order to be active, energetic and successful. The same equation of *aggression = warmongering = activity = energy = maleness = success* is applied to sexual activity, and *male* sexual activity is coupled by word association with *power*. To be sexually active is to be useful, productive, operative, vigorous and *powerful* — and if you are not, then you must be weak, useless, unproductive and *powerless* — in other words *impotent.* To be castrated is to be unmanned, cowardised, devitalised, de-energised, weakened and made effeminate. It is to be robbed of vitality, healthiness, vigour, red-bloodedness, manliness, aggressiveness and bellicosity — it is to be made into a *WOMAN.* Such is man's vision of himself and such is his thoroughly uncomplimentary vision of women.

This is just 'the way things are', you might say, and Thesaurus is merely reflecting those already existing cornball attitudes. True, but as I explained in the last section, the association between power, patriotism, weapons and male sexuality is not only damaging to the individual, it is also potentially VERY dangerous and threatens the whole future of humankind and perhaps, even, the very survival of the earth itself. It is not, therefore, an association that I would have thought anybody in their right mind would have been anxious to applaud by reason of association with "success". On the contrary, I would have thought that anybody who considered themselves a RESPONSIBLE member of society would be actively trying to DISPEL such destructive associations and beliefs. But it is the same with language as it is with everything else and those who uphold the establishment not only feel they have no responsibility towards changing people's attitudes, they feel they have a duty, in the name of their class, to RESIST any attempts to challenge the status quo. It is not surprising, therefore, that those who compile and update (supposedly) such tomes as Thesaurus happily continue to hand down, through the language, the weighted word association of the traditional patriarchal and aristocratic ascendancy. Reading through Thesaurus it is possible to imagine that the 60's never happened and that Victorian morality, in all its repressive, suffocating and hypocritical glory, had remained unchanged and unchallenged for over a hundred years, and that you could walk outside the door and see horse carriages and muffin men. The language of the establishment is still rooted in imperial glory and hankering after the days of yesteryear when people "respected" their betters and sex hadn't been invented; when women, blacks and servants knew their place, Britain won glorious, bloody battles and nobody questioned the superiority of the rich. Those were the days, sigh . . . It seems to me quite obvious whose reflections of society are being fostered and fanned and whose language we are really talking.

Those amongst us who do not share this nostalgia for the past and perhaps are able to see the world from somebody else's point of view other than rich men, should be very careful about getting caught in language traps. If we want to move forward rather than backwards we must take great care in the use of such words as aggression and impotence and watch out for media tricks entailing the use of loaded words with built-in implications. Aggression is such a loaded, overworked word anyway that I would advise against using it at all and find other, more explicit, words to fit the situation. An aggressive business person, for example, could better be described as 'ruthless, greedy, selfish, callous and/or insensitive'; an aggressive woman who does nothing more than to fight back against her oppression could be 'courageous, energetic, active and/or aware'; an aggressive man who gets drunk and beats up his wife could be a pain in the arse. If the word *IS* used, I would advise caution, especially, against implying any connection between aggression and *ENERGY* (as with the aggressive business person) and if anybody else uses it make sure you determine exactly what THEY mean by the word, however unpopular that may be. Extreme caution should be exercised in the use of the word "IMPOTENT" because it carries a built-in association between power and male sexual prowess, while "WIMP" should be avoided AT

ALL COSTS both as a distasteful insult to women and as a dangerous endorsement of "HAWK" politics. Using *MAN*kind instead of *HUMAN*kind and using *HE* to apply to the individual, as though everybody is male unless otherwise stated, is insulting to women and should be left to the cornballs. It is perfectly possible to use s/he or the third person plural, or 'it' for animals if you don't know the sex. Don't refer to God as 'he' because despite arguments by the Church to the contrary this does suggest the masculine gender.

Language, like cornballs, is always way behind the times because the establishment uses it (as it uses the cornballs) as a means of impeding social advancement. The media discredits any attempt by concerned individuals and progressive movements to move away from the present state of injustice by twisting and distorting their ideas and couching them in loaded, message-ridden language that shouts:

> *"Leave it alone — it's propaganda, it's fanatical, it's communist; he's a wimp, she's unnatural, she's strident; they're subversive, infiltrating, disruptive; they're loony lefties, lesbians, revolutionaries, sinister, violent, immoral . . ."*

It is the language of rich, white men under threat.

*"When I give food
to the poor they call
me a saint.*

*When I ask WHY the
poor have no food they
call me a communist"*

*Dom Helder Camara,
Archbishop of Recife
North East Brazil*

*(From Third World calendar 1985
produced by 'New Internationalist')*

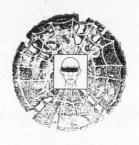

SECTION FIVE

CORNBALL
POWER POLITICS

Everyday politics and power politics may look the same to you and me as we struggle under the yoke of their domination, but for the politicians who are itching for a slice of power and falling over themselves to sell Joe and Joanna public an ideology for the price of a vote, they have a very special significance.

1. IDEOLOGY AND MYTHOLOGY

The Media, politicians and the cornball-in-the-street are exceedingly free with their use of the words "right" and "left" wing — so much so, in fact, that the terms have now acquired so many varied connotations as to be virtually meaningless. What, exactly, do the cornballs think they mean when they look at you and sneer "bloody left-winger" and why do they feel so inordinately proud to be associated with "the right"? It bears investigation, to sift out the myths and identify the ideologies underneath it all. .

Right wing, above all else, means CAPITALISM and capitalism, of necessity, signifies profit, competition, constant material 'growth' and the accumulation of vast amounts of wealth (capital) in the hands of a minority to be used as investments (i.e. to buy up land and the means of production to get other people to work for them and maintain their luxurious life style). The side effects of this system on the human condition are many and varied, nearly all of which are undesirable and destructive — greed, gluttony, sloth, inequality and privilege, to name but a few: and my attempts to document its pernicious effects on the world in general have barely scratched the surface.

Right-wing politicians and those who control the right-wing Media (who invariably come from the upper echelons of society) are understandably not anxious to stress these unsavoury aspects of the system and instead base their propaganda and their sales pitch on well established "right-wing mythology" — which has nothing at all to do with "right-wing ideology". Right-wing mythology states that capitalism provides:—

    ☆ Freedom of choice

    ☆ Equality of opportunity (meritocratic justice) and

    ☆ Freedom of the individual (FREE enterprise, a FREE country)

In reality, none of this is true for anybody except those who have money, and usually comes down to whether or not you have been born into it. If Henry's income — complete with speculations on the stock exchange, tax dodges and interest on inherited capital — is five thousand pounds a week and Pete's is £250 less tax, Pete cannot *CHOOSE* to do most of the things that Henry does because he cannot afford it. There may be a wide range of fee-paying, private schools available but Pete cannot choose ANY of them for his children because he cannot afford them. The freedom for Pete's grown children to choose any of the vast number of private houses on the market is limited by the amount of money they have and if they cannot find the initial deposit to secure a mortgage then NONE will be available to them. Pete may view private medicine as a wonderful means of jumping the National Health queue and getting an operation done on his piles — until he is put out of work and can't afford the premium for the insurance, because then he will have to join the 'welfare' queue for limited, underfunded, medical aid; catch pneumonia in a hospital that can't afford adequate heating, die of a heart attack because the equipment went wrong or watch the blood of one of his children ebb away at the side of the road while waiting for an ambulance that broke down on the way. All the best equipment, brand new ambulances and luxurious private rooms are down the road at the private hospital but Pete couldn't afford the insurance premium, so Pete and his child had to die. Every other "choice" the cornball may care to mention is subject to exactly the same stipulation — if you can't pay for it, the "choice" doesn't exist. The more money you have, the more money you inherit, the more choice will be yours. This may sound puerile and obvious but cornballs DO seem to lose sight of such basic economic facts when waxing lyrical about capitalist "freedom of choice".

The right-wing claim that we have 'equal opportunity' and live in a meritocracy is palpable nonsense and makes the ridiculous assumption that all those at present in control, all those with wealth and position, got there by dint of their own superior efforts in a fair and equal contest. It assumes that inherited wealth, background, education and contacts played no part whatsoever in the final placing of the contestant and all those who are poor, unemployed and in trivial, poorly paid positions — anyone, in fact, who is not in the upper echelons — are not only inferior, they are also fully deserving of their situation because they didn't try hard enough. What appalling arrogance. Do the rich REALLY believe they got there purely through their own efforts? Do they seriously expect *US* to believe it? It is breathtaking in its absurdity, yet the well-fostered myth of 'equal opportunity' still seems to be widespread. Also, the claim itself relies upon the assumption, unchallenged amongst cornballs, that living in a meritocracy is desirable which I, for one, strongly refute. A meritocracy is, after all, just a fancy word for a rat-race in which people are rewarded according to their abilities and would never be a fair race, even if all the participants started off from the same place, because people are not equally endowed with physical and mental capabilities. 'Merit' also begs the question "who decides what constitutes 'merit'?", and which inevitably throws us back into the arms of authority, power structures, division of mental and physical capabilities into different categories of 'worth' to the commercial world, and so on. Back to the position we are in at the moment, in fact, except that we would all start out from scratch, regardless of what our parents had achieved, with no inheritance and no advantages over anybody else. The weak would have to take their chance with the strong, the mentally and physically handicapped with the 'normal'. We would all be taken away from our parents when we had been weaned and brought up in an institution where we would be educated, schooled in the art of vicious and single-minded competition, taught to be ruthless, callous 'pragmatists' and let out the other end to claw our way up the capitalist, meritocratic tree. If we only managed to get one degree we would become manual workers. Two degrees and upwards, managers and administrators. Those who didn't get a degree at all would be considered 'worthless' and if kept alive at all would only be given the bare necessities to exist. I say "we", but would women be included in this meritocratic rat race? Or would they get packed off for a separate education to encourage them to stay out of the job market and be good little housewives to aspiring hubbies? Doubtless. Doubtless, also, the education of those who didn't shape up by the age of twelve would, sooner or later, get neglected and cut short to enable them to take up their positions as poorly paid 'physical' workers without too much resentment. No, it doesn't excite me, this right-wing dream of meritocratic Utopia, even if it WERE feasible — which it isn't. There is certainly a place for working and contributing according to ability, but this would only work within a socialist system that operated for the common good. It could never work in a capitalist system, which necessarily operates in favour of personal greed at the expense of the weaker members of society, and the whole idea of right-wing 'equal opportunity' is a complete farce.

The last of the major levers of right-wing mythology is that capitalism provides for 'freedom of the individual' via 'free enterprise' in a 'free' society. "Land of opportunity" sings America "Defend the free world against communist enslavement and the evil empire". But what does the rhetoric actually MEAN? What does freedom mean to the poor; to blacks; to the unemployed; to battered wives; to child incest victims; to the homeless; to the destitute; to the mentally and physically handicapped; to petty thieves with "form" trying to reshape their lives; to kids in violent family backgrounds; to teenage junkies; to one parent families; to all those in soul-destroying jobs; to all those ruining their health in dangerous and unhealthy working conditions; to those working in tin mines in Bolivia; to those being beaten, tortured and murdered in El Salvador, Chile and Guatemala; to all those who are killed by stress diseases before they reach retirement age; to lonely old people, living out the twilight of their lives cold, malnourished and neglected; to women getting through their days on alcohol and valium; to victims of lung cancer and emphysema; to those killed and maimed in industrial accidents; to wives and families of those killed and maimed in the South Atlantic; to those killed in Vietnam; to poor Catholics in Ulster; to the wrongly convicted in prison; to political prisoners in South Africa; to victims of police brutality the 'free' world over; to animals; to children of the hopeless in the third world; *FREEDOM FOR WHOM . . . TO DO WHAT?* Freedom for anybody with enough money and power to exploit anybody else without it; freedom for employers to use women 'outworkers' as slave labour knowing they can do nothing about it; freedom for whites to terrorize black communities; freedom for husbands to rape and beat wives and children; freedom for multi-nationals to exploit native labour the 'free' world over. Freedom of the *STRONG* over the *WEAK*. Freedom of *WHITES* over *BLACKS*. Freedom of *MEN* over *WOMEN*. Freedom of the *RICH* over the *POOR*. Freedom of the *POWERFUL* over the *POWERLESS*. For *WHOM* is it a *"FREE"* society? For rich, white men . . . and nobody else.

Right-wing ideology — as opposed to right-wing mythology — is the science of how to keep rich men rich, other men working for them, and women in their power — without threats of revolution. In rich countries, where the crumbs are plentiful, it is no problem for the rich to knock enough off the inherited tables to keep the minions off their backs (the trickle down syndrome) and sustain a substantial 'middle class' of aspiring upward-mobiles. In rich countries, it is possible for the rich minority to allow for 'free enterprise' amongst the subordinates and the ensuing rat-race for the crumbs takes their minds off the cake from whence they fell. In rich countries, the rich can allow for a 'democratic' means of electing them, which encourages the masses to believe that whatever happens to them is their own fault because it was they, after all, who 'democratically elected' the bunch who are messing up their lives. (Note the dilemma of the striking miners who were constantly faced with the outcry of the establishment and of their own cornball workmates against 'flying in the face of a democratically elected government'.) The right-wing democratic farce is rooted in the same system of controlled alternatives as every other aspect of right-wing ideology — we, the public, can decide WHICH bunch of power-seekers we want to rule our lives, use our labour and allow a minority to cream off most of the profits in the interests of capital 'investment' and we can determine, to an extent, how MANY crumbs we can expect — but we are not allowed to choose not be be ruled by *ANY* of them and we cannot choose to share out the whole cake. No real choice at all, in fact.

In rich countries, where most of the population is working and being kept quiet with televisions and videos it is possible for the ruling power to keep police intervention to a minimum and for the strong arms of the law and the military to remain dormant, languishing under a disguise of personal and national security against criminals and outside invasion. In poor countries, however, where the crumbs are less plentiful, the story is rather different. In poor countries like El Salvador, Guatemala and Chile, where a large proportion of the population is poverty-stricken and starving, right-wing liberalism (democracy) swiftly becomes right-wing dictatorship (fascism). Minimum police and military intervention becomes maximum control — and free enterprise is limited to scavenging on the municipal rubbish dumps. In poor countries para-military forces, riot squads, torture, police detainment without trial, 'political' prisoners, strict press and TV control and heavy censorship of all literature are all a part of everyday life as a necessary means of preventing uprisings against the inequalities of their right-wing society — a necessary part of safeguarding the profits of the rich. In poor countries right-wing ideology is laid bare for all to see and nobody knows better than the miserable, oppressed peasants of central America the farcical nature of right-wing 'freedom of choice'.

Apart from the home-spun right-wing propaganda there is the well publicized and constantly stoked mythology that East and West are divided by ideology. They are not. They are divided by a common male chauvinism and a common obsession. When I see Reagan and Gorbachev snarling at one another across the third world I do not see two men concerned to uphold an ideology, I see two cockerels fluffing up their plumage, scratching the ground and crowing over their territory — and their hens. I do not see two people concerned about the future of their people, concerned to uphold freedom and principle, concerned about the fate of the earth and its inhabitants — I see two old patriarchs determined to stay in power, determined to uphold phallic superiority and patriarchal values at all costs — even at the expense of the earth and all living creatures. Both East and West are run by men, both are militaristic, both are imperialistic, both are obsessed with the fantasy of masculine omnipotence. As for ideology and the practical working of an economic system, it is undeniable that the vast majority of the Russian people are better off materially under communism than they were under the cruel and exploitative rule of the Tzars and it is arguable that, at least for a time, a centralized power structure with a powerful internal means of control was necessary in order to avoid threats from the rich and powerful of the previous regime — but that no longer applies and the fact that male values still dominate in an otherwise (outwardly) equality-seeking structure and that those male values are at present threatening the whole planet should be a warning to all those who believe that feminism is secondary to the fight for equality. The Soviet system is authoritarian (economic) socialism without individual autonomy and without a feminist perspective; quasi-equality of the male and his masculine values of production and subjugation of the female and her feminine values of **RE**production. The patriarchs of America and the West sell freedom — without equality — and the patriarchs of Russia sell equality — without autonomy. Both are a myth. Both sides act in the primary interests of phallic, minority power — not of the propagandist conceptions of right- and left-wing ideology fabricated by the self-interested for the digestion of the dispossessed. There is no such thing as freedom without equality and vice versa — and NEITHER is possible under a centralized power structure of ANY description, whether it be based on the rich, the aristocrat or the civil servant. The super-power patriarchs of America extol the virtues of Western 'freedom' to their hens and lower orders and spits insults at Russian constraint, while their Russian counterparts tirelessly expound the superior nature of their philanthropic leadership while exploiting every opportunity to illustrate the evils of Western freedoms. Meanwhile, both sides operate internal systems of establishment secrecy that squash hoi-polloi dissent on the grounds of 'endangering national security' (the enemy within, communist plots, bourgeois-capitalist individualism etc. etc.). Both have mental institutions in which those are placed who will not agree, or cannot cope, with the rules of the dominant patriarchs. Both use powerful drugs and psychiatrists (psycho-analysts, psycho-therapists et al) to convince the individual that s/he is at odds with society, not the other way round. Both societies are based on patriotic arrogance, both are wedded to increased industrial output, economics, material growth and division of labour, both are centred around phallic technology (the conquest of nature and women's creative capacity by men and machines — the conquest of the earth by nuclear weapons, the conquest of space by rockets). Both societies are sterile and mechanical, both have forfeited their souls in the interests of male dominance and economics. The fact that women are 'allowed' to dig the roads in Russia for equal return does not mean that they have achieved equality of recognition — it merely means they have been absorbed into a society that is still based on the qualities that **MEN** consider superior. It does not mean that Russian men have conceded anything at all towards accepting women's DIFFERENCES and so-called women's VALUES as being as important and necessary as those associated with men and it does not mean that they have accepted women's creative capacity, the nurturing of children and the running of the home to be of equal importance and spiritual significance as men's machines, men's Gods-of-creation and men's externally created symbols of human beings' intellectual yearning for knowledge; nor is traditional 'women's' work recognised as being worthy of equal monetary reward any more than it is in the West. Women in Russia still do a major part of the unpaid work associated with reproduction while men are rewarded in wages (and hence independence) in their all-important roles as 'producers'. Outside their 'duties' in the home Russian women are being forced to prove they can do the same things, mentally AND physically, as men to establish their right to equal rewards, just as women in the West are expected to prove their 'worth' by becoming one of the guys and striving to better them in their competitive, compassionless world of machines and economics in which spiritual needs and human happiness are sacrificed to the greater God of materialism and the worship of the Golden Calf. If women ruled the world with the same sexual bias I suppose an equivalent would be to say that if men couldn't embroider intricate patterns as exquisitely as women they would be considered inferior. Some men, with small, delicate fingers, would doubtless be as good at it as women — but a large percentage of men, who have a physical propensity towards larger bones, would undoubtedly prove to be inferior. In such a society women would be paid handsomely for housework and child-rearing and for all delicate and intricate work only suitable for delicate, sensitive fingers (like surgery, typing, sewing etc.) while men would be relegated to inferior rewards in such exclusively 'male' occupations as heavy, physical labour. As it is, since the (male created) criterion of superiority is strength (and speed) and given that men, overall, are physically larger and stronger than women then quite obviously women, overall, are going to be viewed as inferior (hence the pressure on women athletes to end up looking like men). Likewise, all the while competition, insensitivity and ruthlessly acquired material success are considered of more worth than co-operation, compassion and life-centred activities like child-rearing then woman, quite apparently, will continue to be made to feel inferior if the latter qualities and domains are exclusively 'HERS'. Women on both sides of the divide do themselves no favours and the world no service by trying to play competitive games in which the rules are weighted and the judges biased, nor by trying to prove to the patriarchs that they can be just as callous, ruthless and intransigent as their male counterparts (to wit M. Thatcher) because this will do nothing to encourage men to display their capacity for sensitivity and co-operation that is at present only associated with the female and will merely make men more convinced that the male vision of excellence is the only one worth aspiring to. It is MEN who must radically change if the world is to survive, not women. It is the male who must be encouraged to put aside his destructive priorities and to be proud of his ability to feel compassion, not the female to be proud of her capacity for ruthlessness. It is the male who must admit that the values he has so scathingly discarded onto the female are the very values that will ensure his own survival and it is HE who must adopt those values as a part of his humanity in order to save us all. It is HE who must adopt his full share of responsibility for nurturing children, for avoiding unwanted pregnancies and for preserving life not SHE who must be forced to forfeit motherhood, have abortions and suffer the death of her children in senseless wars. It is the male who must finally admit to being ashamed of his appalling human rights record, of his narcissistic arrogance towards women, of his callousness and of his blood lust. It is HE who must abandon competition in favour of co-operation, intransigence in favour of understanding, arrogance in favour of humility, slaughter in favour of life. It is the male who must atone for his sins in the name of his father, his son and his soul — not the female. Lysistrata's power was in making men realize their own dependence on women, not in trying to beat them at their own pathetic, warmongering games. Likewise the power of Greenham Common lies in the symbolic gesture of disgust against male dominance and its inevitable, destructive by-products — not in a demonstration of strength — and it would do a lot of good to all those men of peace whose male egos are so sorely distressed at being excluded from it to realize what it is all about. If a group of men were to form a similar group as a symbolic gesture against phallic power, chant such messages as "Thatcher is a prick" and denounce patriarchal values by throwing darts at, or ritually setting alight, an effigy of an erected phallus-cum-nuclear-rocket then I, for one, would heartily applaud them and thoroughly endorse their right for it to remain an entirely male demonstration. I can't help wondering, however, how many Western men would find the courage to make such an admission, any more than I can help wondering how many of those austere Soviet patriarchs would respond to the challenge of tearing down the damaging divide overshadowing Europe to allow the women of East and West a chance to communicate their dissatisfaction. The case, it seems to me, is that the powers that be in the East are just as frightened by the potential power of the women and their own dissident 'left wing' as those of the West, are just as determined to keep them under control and are just as loth to part with their masculine power symbols. It is therefore up to the women of East and West to cross the divide, break down barriers and alter the male attitudes that so destructively dominate the world — and it is up to the men of the left to give them their support — financially, verbally and demonstrably.

The ideology of the left, when freed from super-power connotations, is in reality extremely difficult to define because it rests to a large degree on faith, intangibles and unproven and partially-proven theories and the variety of different ideas that abound within the framework of the broad left are not as simply unravelled as are those of the right (which are manifested within the existing status quo). Socialists, communists, feminists, anarchists, anarcho-feminists, socialist-feminists, national socialists, autonomous socialists — each places different emphasis on what they want and each believes in different priorities as to how to go about getting it. All of those who can realistically call themselves 'left wing' have two things in common, however — we all want to see an end to capitalism and we all want radically to alter the present structure of society to make it more just, more equal and less destructive. This, unfortunately, cannot be said to apply to the majority of our politicians — although on the fringe of the left hover, past and present, a collection of power-seeking, unscrupulous and opportunistic politicians who are — or have been — prepared to use the name of socialism to further their own careers but who in reality have no more sympathy with the ideals of the left than their Tory counterparts. Wilson, Callaghan, Owen, Healey, Jenkins . . . the list in full of right-wing infiltrators would be considerably longer than a similar one would be for those who genuinely believe in radical, left-wing changes to the structure of the present right-wing society. Not many Labour politicians believe in working towards the installation of autonomous socialism (note the hysterical reaction against Peter Tatchell by the Labour leadership at the suggestion of 'extra-parliamentary activity') and most are considerably more interested in the twin obsessions of 'wealth creation' and 'expanding the economy' than in the furtherance of left-wing, humanitarian principles and in the fulfilling of human needs. The theories of successive Labour governments have been seen to hinge upon those of bureaucratic capitalism in which capitalist investment abroad (i.e. third world exploitation), inequality and the rule-of-the-rich still prevailed and whose only claim to deviation from Tory politics was in the nationalization of various home industries and public services — and even those were still permitted to run on traditional manager-worker principles and differentials, were still expected to make a *profit* in the best capitalist tradition and never made any pretentions towards being run solely in the interests of the general public. It is really no wonder so many hitherto faithful socialists amongst the old working class have now abandoned the Labour party and no less surprising that the right wing have gleefully made so much political mileage out of the downfall of what Labour has so shamefully called 'socialist principles'. Those amongst the Labour party whose idea of socialism is bureaucratic capitalism should own up and join the SDP — and allow the party to regain its integrity by re-affirming its original socialist convictions.

The fact that it is impossible to pigeon-hole the vastly differing theories within the left wing under one neat heading has never deterred the right-wing establishment or the cornballs from doing just that. The left wing, they say, are all communists, all looney, all Russian sympathisers and all part of a fiendish plot to take away individual freedom and open the floodgates to rampant bureaucracy and communist dictatorship. This is pure mythology — the ideology of the left as seen through the eyes of the right. It is also pure mythology that the 'right' is morally superior to the 'left', as epitomised in the seemingly immortal associations listed in Thesaurus:—

LEFT	RIGHT
Clumsy, forgotten, sinister, bad, harmful, adverse, frightening, dishonest.	Apt, straight, true, accurate, virtuous, good, white, guiltless, irreproachable, worthy, praiseworthy, noble, philanthropic, right handed, decent, normal, moral, upright.

This view of right and left is one that the establishment works very hard to keep alive in order to ridicule and discredit anybody who threatens to make changes to the present system. It is painfully obvious, however, that the present status quo is not virtuous, good, philanthropic, moral and praiseworthy, it is cruel, exploitative, selfish, greedy and thoroughly BAD — as are all those on the right who are so determined to uphold it. Those on the left are not sinister, bad, harmful and dishonest, they are basically people who are concerned, alarmed and disgusted by the present system and its effects on the world and want to do something to change it for the better — and it is high time Thesaurus, the right-wing establishment and the cornballs were made to face up to the truth.

INDUSTRIAL
MANUFACTURING NORTH
(the colonial powers of old)

HEADED BY SUPER POWER U.S.A.

PRICES CONTROLLED BY WORLD ECONOMIC SYSTEM IN FAVOUR OF CHEAP RAW MATERIALS AND EXPENSIVE MANUFACTURED GOODS

AGRICULTURAL AND RAW MATERIAL SOUTH
(the colonised lands of old imperialist powers now referred to as the third world)

TEA, COFFEE, MINERALS, EXOTIC FRUIT, TIMBER, ETC...
produced with cheap, black, non-union labour by rich-world multi-nationals funded by rich-world capital, largely for rich-world consumption. These 'investments' make fortunes for rich-world speculators and provide pensions for rich-world inhabitants in their old age. No such pensions or fortunes reach workers in tin mines or coffee plantations.

FREE MARKET ZONES IN INDUSTRIALIZED COUNTRIES, *in which global big business uses cheap labour (often women) to manufacture and market goods. Countries that let in transnational investment will become new additions to the third world (under American domination) prior to the establishment of the new order of global wealth v global poverty. The European Common Market, together with USA military installations and NATO have already set the stage.*

COMMON TRAITS OF THIRD WORLD COUNTRIES.

1. Providers of cheap, non-unionised labour for the rich.

2. Dictatorships and Police States.

3. Low value currencies making them tourist havens for rich foreigners to live in styles far beyond the means of the majority of the native populations.

4. Providers of cheap "Bargain" goods for rich foreigners to take home to show their friends. (It used to be Mexican ponchos, now it's Wedgwood China).

5. Characterised by a minority of very rich, a limited middle class and an impoverished majority.

6. Semi-American cultures with beef-steaks and high technology medical care that only the minority can afford, plus 'Dallas' with sub-titles to inspire free enterprise and instil aspirations for a swimming pool into the starving.

7. Dominated by American business interests; political systems dictated by the White House.

2. THIRD WORLD BRITAIN

Cornballs, as I've said before, don't like change and if everything could go along just as it is they would be quite happy, regardless of who had to suffer in the process. Change, however, is an integral part of the capitalist system. Capitalism can never be stagnant because it relies on constant feeding, constant re-organization, constant acceleration and a constant search for new markets. There is no real security under capitalism because it is a constant round of competition, job-cutting, antagonism and changes of fortune. Nobody amongst those who are fighting for crumbs ever really knows who is going to be the next victim, the next redundant, the next bankrupt — or what product is going to be obsolete in a year's time. Predictions in the market place are as uncertain as next week's weather and no country can ever guarantee that it is not going to be the next victim of capitalist economics.

Throughout these pages I have talked about rich worlds and poor worlds, industrialised countries and cash crop countries, the privileged and the under privileged. I have painted (or tried to) an international picture of capitalist economics and tried to show how it works to the advantage of the few and the detriment of the majority. I have tried to show how poor countries, by having their land turned over to cash crops to serve the needs of richer peoples, thereby become dependent upon expensive, imported food to survive, which then goes to the rich of their own countries and leaves many of the poor to starve. I have tried, similarly, to give the reader a picture of the way in which the dictators in much of the poor world exploit the people of their countries to obtain luxury imported goods for the rich while neglecting and oppressing the poor. I hope that I have imparted in the process a general understanding of the way in which multi-nationals exploit the peoples of poor countries by using them as cheap labour and extracting the resources of their lands for their own profit. I have tried to give an overall impression of the way the rich-world habit of relying on animal produce for protein is a minority indulgence and extremely wasteful of precious agricultural land needed to feed the peoples of the world. I hope I have conveyed a general vision of the world as a dependent whole, in which big business (in the form of multi-national trading conglomerates) is carving up the world and using its people as cheap labour to extract its resources in the interests of making a few people very rich and very powerful — because this is what is happening. Sovereign states and independent nations with influential governments are becoming a thing of the past, and governments are being used more and more in the interests of big business, in the interests of the market place, in the interests of the world's rich. Governments are becoming a mere tool of rich business men of the world to oppress the world's poor and exploit the world's labour force. Multi-nationals shift money backwards and forwards across frontiers and borders via the world's banks as though they didn't exist, and humanitarian leaders are frequently defeated by the inordinate power invested in the holders of capital. Democracies are becoming a thing of the past, an outdated concept, and governments are being instated by the conglomerate power of big business; policies dictated by the requirements of the market place (market forces). Third world countries (like Nicaragua) that try to escape from the iron clutches of foreign business domination and instate socialist systems of national independence are browbeaten, threatened and (sooner or later) brought to heel by imperialist powers protecting their business interests (don't be fooled by all that crap about 'communist infiltration'). If the people of a country try to demand more money for their labour, multi-nationals can merely move, or threaten to move, their companies somewhere else where they can get cheaper labour, and they are in an ever more unchallengeable position to call the tune on the price of labour *WORLD WIDE*. The multi-nationals are fast becoming the world dictators with a stranglehold over resources — including food; and they operate entirely in the name of the rich at the expense of freedom and autonomy — at the expense of people's lives and well being — and with weaponry, militarism and dictatorial tactics the built-in necessities of their expansionist mode of operation. Multi-nationals are the 20th century colonists: invading armies given a veneer of respectability under the guise of international capitalism.

122

Throughout previous pages I have associated Britain with the rich, exploitative industrialised north — but this is not a stable, GUARANTEED position and if I were a cornball I would be starting to get extremely alarmed, along with the rest of us, about what has been happening in Britain since the oil crisis. Recessions are not acts of God or unavoidable parts of the natural order of things, as the right wing would like us to believe, they are an unavoidable and inevitable part of the man-made phenomenon known as capitalism — and this latest recession is just another example of the unworkability of the system. Prior to the oil crisis the industrialized countries had been exploiting the (now) OPEC countries and stealing their oil via rich world multi-nationals so that we could all have cheap energy. After the oil crisis — when the oil-producing countries seized control of their own oilfields — things went rapidly downhill. Since we had all, by that time, organized our economies around recciving cheap energy from afar, it came as a terrible shock when we had to start paying a fair price for it. This had the effect of throwing the rich-world countries into fierce competition with one another to keep from going under and the battle is still going on to establish 'the new order'. Unfortunately for Britain, low on marketable, manufacturable resources and high on import dependency — the 'new order' looks none too promising. Britain, like many other industrialized nations, is highly vulnerable to the effects of recessions caused by poorer countries taking control of their own resources because we have allowed ourselves to become so dependent upon them, and even if there were some way of wriggling out of the present crisis — which there isn't — another one would inevitably follow hard on its heels. As we all know, the standard right-wing answer to 'recovery' is to become 'more competitive' — but the only way to do that is to put even **MORE** people out of work and insist that workers take huge cuts in wages. Thatcher's problem as a right-wing politician is that she can't oppress the majority hard enough or fast enough, due to the irksome necessity of appearing to conform to the demands of our so-called democratic system and without risking outright rebellion amongst the unionised work force. What she would dearly love to do (and she's made no secret of it) is to render unions powerless so that she can offer nice, cheap labour to foreign investors; and the next step would be to do away with all the 'expensive and unnecessary' handouts — like social security benefits, the dole, child allowances etc. — that are responsible for 'bringing the country to its knees' and provide industry with a reserve labour bank of semi-starving and impoverished people who would be eager and willing to work for any kind of pittance they could get. This, of course, would necessitate a greatly increased police force with much greater powers than it now has to control an angry and poverty-stricken population, coupled with a private army (riot squads) to control rebellions and ensure the safety of the rich, ruling minority. Meanwhile, she would continue to be committed to attracting foreign investment any way she could in order to uphold the living standards of that same minority — and since we don't have much in the way of marketable, natural resources for multi-nationals to exploit our only use to foreign investors would be to provide the cheap labour necessary to manufacture and market the raw materials they had obtained dirt-cheap elsewhere. Of course we DO have a good climate for growing crops so our countryside could be churned up to produce cash crops to export in exchange for such imported goods as Argentine beef — a luxury indulgence for the rich — and other luxury items far beyond the pockets of the impoverished majority. She would, this iron lady, be perfectly happy to sell out the majority of the people of this country as cheap labour and allow the countryside to be turned over to two or three cash crops to obtain foreign currency as a means of buying imported luxuries. She would be happy for foreign multi-nationals increasingly to move in and make use of the country and its people and for us to become a country with no manufacturing industry of our own, no means of survival beyond that of cash crops and entirely dependent on foreign investment; a nation dependent for its whole survival on the whims of the rich in other countries, dictated to by big business interests, no bargaining power to demand a fair price for our crops, no power to demand a living wage for our labour and unable to break our dependence on the power of the international market and the one-sided economic bias in favour of richer countries. She would be happy to turn this country over to foreigners and to use the population of the whole country to maintain the privileged life style of the world's rich. And when we were sick and tired of our oppression, poverty and hopelessness and tried to break free from the international market place and the iron grip of foreign investors she would not need to call in an imperialist foreign power to help her quell the rebellion, it is already *HERE*, ready and willing as ever to "keep out the scourge of communism" and spread alarmist right-wing propaganda around rich-world Western countries to ensure that they gave us no support.

If you think I am being alarmist as part of a 'communist plot', or if you believe 'it can't happen here', just take a look around you and see what is going on. Already the only difference between large parts of Northern Ireland, Scotland, Wales and the North of England and emergent industrialized nations of the third world like Brazil is the welfare state and that, as we all know, is under all kinds of threat. Already our home industries are well on the way to being defunct. Already Margaret Thatcher has sold off half the country to private industry and thrown essential services at the mercy of vested interests and profiteering. Already high-street supermarkets are becoming huge out-of-town super-stores and hypermarkets monopolising whole areas, sending small businesses to the wall and effectively dictating work opportunities (and conditions) to whole communities. Already the police are being given more and more power and are ever less accountable for their actions. Already, under the guise of 'cleaning up' television and videos, censorship threatens to vastly diminish freedom of expression in a variety of areas — including that of political dissent. Already the unions have had their powers eroded and diminished and during the miners' strike workers had their right to picket seriously threatened and were even prevented from moving freely from one part of this 'free' country to another. To quote from a leaflet published by the NCCL (National Council for Civil Liberties):—

Since that time (February 1984) . . .

☆ The Police and Criminal Evidence Bill has been passed giving the police unprecedented powers;

☆ Computerised National Insurance 'identity' cards have been introduced;

☆ Telephone tapping in Britain has been found to contravene the European Convention on Human Rights;

☆ Trade unions were banned at GCHQ Cheltenham;

☆ Sarah Tisdall was imprisoned for 6 months;

☆ A "Data Protection" Act has been passed which fails to adequately protect personal privacy;

☆ By-laws were changed and a road widened to stifle dissent at Greenham Common;

☆ Alternative bookshops have been raided and stocks seized.

Does this overall picture of Thatcherite Britain, coupled with the spectacle of the countryside being churned up to produce wheat mountains and oil seed rape not trigger the ringing of alarm bells? How much further does it have to go before the people of this country wake up to the fact that we are being turned into a third world country for the benefit of the rich? Already, the world has moved into the final stages of capitalism under which, eventually, there will be no such thing as sovereign states and the world will belong entirely to big business. Every country, to a lesser or greater degree, will be run along the same lines as Chile and El Salvador — headed by puppet dictators and comprised of a minority of very rich and a majority of very poor, starving and oppressed. The extended middle class, free enterprise and ELECTED dictators (right-wing democracy) will all be things of the past and para-military forces, atrocity, torture, detention without trial, 'disappearances', political prisoners and heavy censorship of the press, television and all literature — will be common factors of everyday life. There will be no (effective) trades unions and no worthwhile welfare states, and big businessmen will dictate the terms of our employment in order that they make the maximum profits. Rich and poor countries will gradually disappear and the world will become one entity, with a rich minority plundering its resources at an ever increasing pace and using a dispossessed poor majority as cheap labour.

The means of avoiding this nightmare situation is not, as right-wing politicians in all parties claim, to become MORE competitive in the world market place and the emphasis should not be placed on "wealth creation" and "economic recovery". The answer is not MORE capitalism because that can only lead to MORE multi-nationals, bigger and bigger businesses with ever greater power and an ever more impenetrable monopoly (and, paradoxically for the liberal right wing, less and less competition), to MORE exploitation and more nuclear lunacy. The only possible answer to our problems is less competition and more co-operation (as opposed to less competition and more conglomerate monopolies), less economic/material growth and more self-sufficiency/NEGATIVE growth, less capitalism and more socialism, less economic dependence on market forces and more national independence. There is absolutely NO point in expecting to escape from this present situation by using the remedies of the past because they just won't work. There are no new empires to build, no more lands left to ravage and exploit; we are into a whole different ball game now and it is a lot more serious than anything that has gone before. It is no earthly use the Labour party clinging to the old notions of capitalist philanthropy because as M. Thatcher realizes — and a good deal better than all the woolly right-wing liberals in her own and other parties — the days of right-wing philanthropy towards the lower orders are over. If capitalism is to be kept alive in this country, and if the rich are to maintain their wealth, their power and their privileges, then the old ideas of a mixed economy and a welfare state have got to go. This country will never again be a great power and will never again be able to afford to give liberal hand-outs to the masses. These are not 'temporary' austerity measures we are experiencing, they are *PERMANENT*, and they will get *WORSE*. The Labour party, if re-elected, will find no answers to this dilemma if it doggedly insists upon clinging to right-wing policies in the misguided belief that it can somehow pluck money out of the air to provide all the community benefits that the Tories are hard at work taking away. No doubt the right-wing members of the Labour party still fondly believe they could avoid committing themselves to left-wing policies by borrowing huge sums of money to prop up the 'mixed' economy, but this would inevitably prove as fruitless as it has for Brazil and all the other countries who believed in living on the never-never. Sooner or later the bills have to be paid and sooner or later the austerity measures would return with a vengeance. In any case, it is lunacy to believe that we can go ON plundering the resources of the earth to produce ever more consumer rubbish, ever more pollution and ever more tons of waste; go ON belching fumes into the atmosphere and waste into the oceans with a total disregard for the balances of nature that ensure our continued survival; go ON producing dangerous nuclear waste that will remain deadly for thousands of years to come. We have got to STOP being so diabolically irresponsible and start to take care of our precious earth, the creatures that live on it, the people we share it with and the atmosphere that surrounds it. The only hope of 'recovery' for this country — as it is for the world — lies with taking a responsible attitude towards the environment and towards each other, with adopting a frugal attitude towards our resources and learning to use as *LITTLE* as possible instead of greedily trying to grab, grasp, consume and devour as *MUCH* as possible, and it lies with achieving national and individual autonomy and national self-sufficiency.

If the people of this country are serious in their claims to wanting a free, just and equal society and if they genuinely want to see a return of a 'Great' Britain that they can feel proud to belong to and which will provide a beacon to the rest of the world — then they have got to put in a lot of hard work and be prepared to undergo a drastic transformation of character, habits, aspirations and political outlook. The alternatives will be much, much worse — and there's very little time left to make the choice.

SECTION SIX

CONCLUSIONS

Much has been claimed by right-wing politicians and cornballs about how much better off we all are than we were a hundred years ago, and in terms of material possessions I've no doubt most of it is true. A hundred years ago we didn't have televisions, food mixers, electric toothbrushes and videos, for sure, because they hadn't been invented. Nobody could deny that central heating, social security, regular food and warm clothes have improved our standard of living with regard to the material comfort of our lives, but what of the *QUALITY* of our lives? Are we healthier or happier? Are we freer or more equal? Are we more autonomous, more in control of our lives, more able to cope with life? What does QUALITY mean?

I once read a book called *'Los Viejos'* (The Old Ones) which was the story of the day-to-day lives of a group of peasants living in a small village high up in the Andes of Ecuador and set in a beautiful green valley with clean air and an almost constant temperature of around 70 degrees F. The peasants lived under the 'hacienda' system (a fancy name for feudalism) and had to work a large field for the landlord in return for a small plot for themselves and their families. There was no money system and the landlord paid in seeds, animals and the use of his land, but not with a salary. The peasants were dirt-poor and worked long hours for the privilege of living in a mud hut and making the landlord rich. This was my first impression, regardless of the sensitivity with which the author, Grace Halsell, sketched the reality of the day-to-day lives of the peasants. My mind would not move beyond the anger I felt at the fact of them being exploited.

"It's all very well going on about their dignity and the majesty of toil," I thought "but if that bastard wasn't sitting on his backside reaping all the benefits of their majestic toil they'd be a damn sight better off". So I didn't really get a lot from the book at the time and put it away thinking she was just one more patronising American, content to look upon the poor as "such beautiful, REAL people" while she went back to yachts and private planes in the USA and robbed the 'REAL' people blind. A few years ago, however, I went to Central America and it made me rethink my Westernised, rich-world concepts about poverty. Gradually, the lives of those peasants of Vilcabamba, high up in the Andes, began to take on a different significance. So I re-read Grace Halsell's book and her words struck chords of recognition with me as I recalled the attitude of poverty-stricken peasants I had encountered all over Central America. Time and again I found myself confronted with the concepts of autonomy and pride; of sharing, caring, loving and co-operation. Below are a few passages from the book which I hope will clarify the points I want to make:

Visitors to Vilcabamba claim there is 'something special' about the valley, and yet the 'Viejos' are in many respects like millions of dirt-poor country folk; hardworking, uncomplicated and relatively serene.

Through stern physical labour they have earned for themselves a self-respect and sense of fulfillment missing in many urban lives. They are as one with the soil, as native to the earth as a seed of corn. Nature's cycle governs their lives, from the green promise of spring to the mature ripeness of autumn. Age has mellowed and enriched them. Modern victims of the myriad distractions and demands of our industrial society might conclude that the Viejos are bored with the profound simplicity of their lives. But it is not true. They are renewed by the changing seasons, the process of growth in which they participate as energetic allies.

They live hard, sparse, lives and in earthly goods they are well below the poverty line.

They know nothing of politics. The economics of their existence is measured in what they earn to feed and clothe themselves. Their large dramas centre on affairs of the human heart.

Señora Mariana Toledo had never been to a beauty salon, never used lipstick, powder or rouge. But time had not robbed her of an inner radiance and her smile suggested that her husband found her an attractive mate. She was thin, with acute faculties, good vision, good hearing, a clear mind and an excellent memory. She was independent, even tempered, possessed of a lively humour and found it easy to laugh.

. . . most of us are not concerned with 'forever' as much as we are interested in learning how to stay active and useful and happy, let's say up to 100. I went to learn from the Viejos, because they had lived longer than any other known group in this Western hemisphere. And most important, they are still working, and loving and lovable, and — what pleases me most of all — they spend a lot of their time laughing.

Now it would be all too easy to start waxing lyrical about the beauty and simplicity of their lives and forget about the sheer grind of their daily battle to stay alive. Also, I have not lost sight of the repugnant fact of the landlord and his power over their lives and I'm not about to forgive or condone his exploitation of their labour any more than I am about to forget the unrelenting, daily fear suffered by the peasants of Central America. There are, however, things to be learnt from people like the Vilcabambans and lessons to be absorbed about the nature of our own life style in the affluent west. In Grace Halsell's words:

"They are active, alive and LOVING people". How many of us are active, alive and LOVING people?

They are **"hardworking, uncomplicated and relatively serene".**

They are **"as one with the soil and governed by Nature's**

cycle. . . . Age has mellowed and enriched them". How many of those things are true of us in our rich world? Many of us are bored, many unemployed and not too many of us serene. We are alienated from natural phenomena and from our true selves. We are set against one another in futile competition and are often greedy, envious, resentful and hostile. Age more often leads to dependence, loneliness and alienation than it does to enrichment. Where, then, did we lose our way? Where did we lose our self-esteem and our 'loving' natures? How have we strayed so far from our selves and our spirits as to make us so ailing and soul-less? It is not a difficult question to answer if you consider the pattern of our lives. The moment we are born we are fitted with a label and we are treated according to the information on that label throughout our whole lives. The label reads: CLASS: COLOUR: SEX and once the details are filled in the whole machinery of rich-world politics is set in motion. Society's expectations for us are already determined, our freedom to choose already usurped and curtailed. Our share of the world's resources, the amount of power we will be allowed, our limited choices of career, the amount of respect we can expect throughout our life, the limits of our hopes and dreams — all have already been allocated and any attempt to alter any of them, any small indication that the label may be tampered with, will be met by resistance, hostility and disapproval from the upholders of the status quo. All our lives we see unobtainable carrots dangling in front of us and all around us inequality taunts us into believing that we are inferior and that others, through luck, guile or superiority are better off than we are. Our whole society is built around — depends upon — dissatisfaction. We are constantly encouraged to be dissatisfied with what we have, never to be content, in order to make us want more and more consumer items. Is it any real wonder that our lives feel so empty most of the time, that we so easily become bored and discontented and that we find it increasingly more difficult to 'love our neighbours'? No, not really. Nor is it any more difficult to see why we are undergoing a 'spiritual crisis' that the established Church, with its Victorian vision of morality, is totally unable to deal with.

The fact is that our obsession with materialism has led us into almost total spiritual bankruptcy and no amount of condemnation of sexual activity by the Church is going to make the situation any better. We have allowed our greed for televisions, videos and gourmet food to take priority over our concern for our fellow human beings, over our compassion for other creatures and over our consciences — and we are suffering for it in the loss of all the things that the poor of the world still hold dear; love, co-operation, community spirit, self-esteem, peace with God . . . and a clear conscience.

Our spiritual salvation lies in ensuring that our everyday lives reflect our vision of morality — and that vision must act in accordance both with individual human needs and with the survival of the species (and, indeed, the planet). Loving another human being, whoever it is, cannot be said to be 'sinful' and sexual intercourse (provided, needless to say, it is mutually desired) is a natural expression of that love. It is therefore ludicrous in the extreme to base the greater part of our conception of morality around sexual relationships and equally ludicrous to stipulate that the act of love-making be given the 'blessing of God' ONLY when it is perpetrated with the singular aim of reproduction and ONLY when it is performed between members of opposite genders. Such preoccupation with other people's sex life is bizarre, and quite meaningless as a yardstick of moral or immoral behaviour. It is, on the other hand, *HIGHLY* immoral to kill, torture, abuse and exploit our brothers and sisters on the earth and highly immoral to support, by our actions, inaction and daily activities, a system which allows — nay, encourages — these things to continue, and which runs in dangerous opposition to the survival of the species. The concept of 'unlimited material growth' (i.e. slavish adherence to the dictates of Market Forces) is unworkable and irresponsible — and if God has provided us with a guideline by which to map out our lives it is in the built-in retribution that we invite by flying in the face of Nature and trying to defy its laws. If we want to survive we must learn to live within the limits imposed by the earth's finite resources and by the limited capacity of the environment to compensate for the abuses it is being subjected to — which in itself will provide us with a much-needed boundary of possibilities. A substantial part of the malaise of our time stems from the outwardly LIMITLESS nature of the consumer society, which not only undermines personal responsibility for self-restraint, it also destroys individual sense of purpose. Choices become agonisingly difficult and individual confidence in the moral worth of a decision, when built-in guidelines and constraints have been swept away, becomes increasingly shaky. I see women with brimming supermarket baskets staring trance-like at rows of multi-coloured tins, racks of exotic fruit and freezers full of every kind of meat and every new instant meal on the market — and thinking dazedly 'what on EARTH shall we have for dinner?' Choice, by its very abundance, has become counterproductive. In the days when we had to eat what was available in season, not only were the choices easier and more significant, but variety was guaranteed by Nature's very limitations. We had warming stews with root vegetables in winter, refreshing green salads in summer and fresh fruit straight from the tree. Now we have strawberries at Christmas, sprouts in mid-summer and sweetcorn at Easter. Now we have everything, all year round — and NOTHING to look forward to. When human society reaches the point where money offers a white card for limitless, selfish greed and the lack of it is the only curb on pitiless exploitation and unrestrained self-indulgence, then Hubris reigns and Nemesis merely bides her time.

In order to move away from our present spiritually, morally and ecologically disastrous course, to regain some of our lost integrity and put some dignity back into the human condition I believe we must work in the direction of a) national autonomy and self-sufficiency and b) individual autonomy. With regard to the former, it is conceivable that one day the peoples of the earth will learn to share resources between them in a responsible manner without destroying each other and exhausting the earth in the process, but at the moment it is much more realistic to work towards self-sufficiency on a national basis — and hope that others will follow — and I believe that in the process of doing this we can reduce our problems to manageable proportions and thence regain individual control of the events that shape our lives instead of feeling overwhelmed by the huge powers that seem to swamp and render useless our individual efforts. In this endeavour I believe we must press for national policies that move in the following directions, and for a party that is prepared to implement them:—

☆ To use our own natural resources to the full — without recourse to foreign investment, foreign manufactured goods, foreign raw materials or foreign, home-operated multi-nationals — to feed, clothe, house and raise the whole population to a level of reasonable comfort.

☆ To begin a national research programme into ways in which to harness the natural energy of sun, wind and water to provide us with power.

☆ To use coal to the full, in conjunction with a de-sulphurization programme to minimise acid rain.

☆ To free North Sea Oil and gas from control by foreign investors.

☆ To halt further plans for nuclear power.

☆ To rid our soil of foreign imperialist powers and free ourselves from the death-alliance with foreign nuclear weaponry.

☆ To free ourselves from NATO and leave the Common Market.

☆ To provide a vastly improved public transport system to be used in place of the private car in order to save fuel, cut down pollution and increase freedom of movement.

☆ To make better use of railways as a means of distributing goods in order to improve the quality of the environment.

☆ To begin a national agricultural programme that will allow us to feed ourselves without recourse to imported goods. This will entail the extensive planting of a variety of grains, pulses and vegetables and a minimum reliance upon animal protein. It will also entail extensive research both into the most suitable crops to use and into how to farm them organically, without reliance upon chemicals, together with sympathetic consideration for our dwindling wild life and its natural habitats.

☆ To free ourselves from any connections with the world currency market.

☆☆☆ The entire programme to work in conjunction with a programme to use all our resources for the benefit of the whole population.

Since I believe that none of the present parties can ever be relied upon to do ANY of these things to any significant degree, it will be necessary to form a new one that will be dedicated to the aims of autonomous socialism and whose manifesto will be based on the principles required to bring it to fruition. Now I appreciate that it may seem like a contradiction in terms to talk about a political party being used to implement autonomy, in any form, and if we were to allow ourselves to rely entirely upon that as a means of achieving it then it would certainly prove to be so. However, given that the present status quo is built on a powerful set of self-interests that will not lightly be relinquished and given that we ARE horribly enmeshed in the global wheelings and dealings of an international power structure we MUST have the political power, initially, to break free. This does not mean, though, that we have to go out of the frying pan of one power structure into the fire of another and the means of avoiding this rests upon the second priority that I mentioned, namely that of INDIVIDUAL AUTONOMY. We must, as a nation, strive to be comprised of INFORMED individuals who can participate in the decisions that will affect our lives and who cannot be duped and manipulated by the propaganda churned out by an unscrupulous, self-interested minority, as is the case at present. If we are to rid ourselves, once and for all, from control by bodies of power, elected or otherwise, we must make an effort to become a nation of responsible human beings with an extensive awareness of what is going on around us and a personal commitment to our own welfare, the welfare of our fellow creatures and the condition of the environment. There are many ways this can be done and a wealth of different contributions that the individual can make towards obtaining a better world, some of which are listed below (and many of which are interchangeable).

A. **Adopt a responsible attitude towards your personal and your children's health**

☆ Move away from junk foods towards health foods.

☆ Move away from animal protein towards plant protein.

☆ Move away from powerful drugs towards gentler remedies, especially for minor ailments.

☆ Give up, or cut down, smoking if you possibly can and control intake of alcohol.

☆ Don't give sweets to children or encourage them to eat junk for the sake of control or convenience.

☆ Read about alternative and preventive medicine and be informed about your own body.

☆ Press for such things as organic farming and become involved, generally, in the health food movement and your own health.

☆ Keep up with environmental issues and ORGANISE in your workplace to ensure that it is safe and healthy (according to your own standards and experience, not of self-interested employers or their specially employed 'experts').

B. **Become informed about what is going on in the world — and close to home**

☆ Read *The Guardian* in place of other daily newspapers; perfect it ain't, but it does have some good features, Steve Bell and a decent crossword — and doesn't rely solely on tits and right-wing propaganda (although caution is required with the news coverage, once you've re-arranged the copy into flowing order). Read *The Mirror* in preference to *The Sun.*

☆ Read *"New Internationalist",* an excellent monthly magazine giving a world perspective on current issues.

☆ Read *"Spare Rib"* for a change instead of *"Woman's Own"* (et al).

☆ Make an effort and read some 'alternative' books — if you don't know the other side of the story you can't possibly be so convinced you are right (as opposed to wrong!). "Compendium" bookshop in Camden has a good selection if you are in London. If not, look around. It could open up a whole new world.

For those who are interested in a beyond-the-establishment viewpoint, I would particularly recommend the following:—

How Children Learn: John Holt

How Children Fail: John Holt

Escape from Childhood: John Holt

Patriarchal Attitudes: Eva Figes

Words and Women: Casey Miller and Kate Swift

Natural Disasters, Acts of God or Acts of Man? Anders Wijkman & Lloyd Timberlake

Silent Spring: Rachel Carson (Still pertinent after all these years)

The Ragged Trousered Philanthropists (Still pertinent after all these years) by Robert Tressell

Only One Earth: Barbara Ward and René Dubos

About Men: Phyllis Chesler

Food for a Future: Jon Wynne-Tyson

State of Seige: Jim Coulter, Susan Miller and Martin Walker

Limits to Medicine: Ivan Illich. (I personally find all the work of Illich a bit heavy going, but it is well worth persevering)

☆ *"City Limits"* is the best of its kind, has some good articles and is well worth buying just for the television reviews of Kathy Myers.

☆ *"Monochrome"* is a monthly newspaper well worth its modest 10p.

☆ Read *the 'Morning Star'* for better news coverage than you'll get in the right-wing press (or at least to get the other side of the story).

☆ Don't turn off television documentaries on world atrocities and social 'problems' just because you are convinced in advance that they will be boring, because you want to pretend they don't exist or because you believe you can't do anything about them, anyway. Learn to make a conscious effort to put your own interpretation on the events they deal with rather than rely solely on the one being pushed by the voice in the background. View television news with scepticism — or don't watch it at all. Watch more Channel 4 and less ITV if you want to be better informed.

☆ Talk, discuss, LISTEN — and learn what other people are saying.

C. **Take personal responsibility for your actions and remember that your habits and daily activities affect millions of other people, other creatures and the environment. With this in mind:**

☆ Don't buy *ANY* goods from South Africa — supporting South African trade means supporting South African atrocities.

☆ Try to buy local produce, goods manufactured in Britain and, wherever possible, with home-produced raw materials. Reliance on out-of-season fruit and vegetables from third world countries keeps them in a position of economic dependence on cash crops and provides a disincentive for the rich to plant subsistence crops. Similarly, try to do without — or cut down drastically — tea, coffee, cocoa, sugar, tinned fruit — and all other foreign produce. Stick to British manufactured goods wherever possible — even if they are more expensive or of slightly inferior quality. Remember that the only reason a lot of foreign goods are cheaper is because they have been produced by a poorly paid, non-unionised workforce — often verging on slave labour. Do not support this kind of international price war — it will rebound on you when YOU are the ones who make up the cheap labour for the benefit of rich consumers elsewhere.

☆ Don't buy shares and if you have any, get rid of them. Overseas 'investment' and wheeler-dealer speculation means making money out of other people's labour and other people's misery (usually in the third world).

☆ Don't tell, or laugh at, racist jokes — they are offensive, dangerous and irresponsible. Belittling blacks in this country leads to daily tragedy — and to the abuse of a set of people who, remember, only came here in the first place through colonial intervention (some as a result of slavery, some because they were ASKED to come when we needed cheap labour to run our public transport and national health system) and who only continue to want to come here because the neo-colonialism of rich-world multi-nationals is bleeding their native countries dry and producing a poverty-stricken and aimless population. All too many of them would be only too pleased to 'go back home' if conditions there were better — if only to escape from the disgraceful abuse they are subjected to by the cornballs in this country.

Irish jokes are not funny, they represent the vicious

and calculated strategy of the British ruling class to discredit and ridicule the Irish people and make it appear that the Irish 'problem' continues through their own stupidity and not, as is really the case, through imperialist exploitation and vested interests.[1]

Jewish jokes, don't forget, helped to lay the foundations for the holocaust in the last war. Very droll.

Sexism is no more forgivable, and to all those cornballs who think telling sexist jokes is clever or amusing I say this:

Next time you are sniggering over a pathetic joke that belittles women by making them appear stupid or inferior, and next time you are leering over page 3 of *The Sun* or throwing darts at a pin-up on the wall remember this — This is the kind of disrespect with which you are encouraging OTHER men to treat YOUR wife, YOUR girlfriend, YOUR mother and YOUR daughter and if any one of them is raped, beaten, abused or murdered don't pretend to be shocked or outraged because YOU were a contributory factor. . .

. . . and to all those cornball women who encourage men by laughing at sexist jokes or heaping scorn on the women's movement I say this: Remember that YOU, your daughter, your mother — even your grandmother — could be the next victim of men's disrespect for your feelings, your dignity and your rights.

☆ Buy "Beauty without Cruelty" cosmetics (or equivalents) from wholefood shops and don't support appeals for medical research unless they state that they don't experiment on animals.

☆ Don't stereotype children, treat them as individuals and give them a fighting chance to be happy — and never forget that de-sensitised little boys become men without conscience or pity, little boys who mock little girls become men who rape women.

1. *As a mental exercise, eliminate the red herrings "Catholic" and "Protestant" from the arena of the Irish conflict and try to find another way of defining the protagonists. Republicans v Loyalists? (A power conflict, with little benefit accruing to the Ulster majority which ever way it goes.) Irish v English? (Surely they are ALL Irish?) Or is it REALLY a case of Ulster privileged v Ulster oppressed, with a strong dose of neo-colonial investment from across the water? America has its Nicaragua. . .*

D. **Live simply, so that others may simply live . . .**

Adopt a frugal and responsible 'waste not want not' approach to life and move away from a consumer attitude towards one of subsistence. Waste and extravagance are **_CRIMINALLY SELFISH_** acts in a world of diminishing resources. The accumulation of vast wealth is a moral outrage in a world where people starve, and the hoarding of land and property is a disgrace when fellow humans are homeless and destitute. The perpetrators of such acts are not to be envied, admired or emulated, merely abolished. They are despicable. So . . .

☆ Make full use of what you have and don't throw away anything until it is no longer functional. Look after clothes and do not get trapped into slavishly following trends and fashions — they are expensive, manipulative, wasteful and unnecessary. 'Style' cannot be bought, it has to be earned.

Pass on children's clothes, or swop with friends. Take clothes you have outgrown or 'gone off' to jumble sales or give them away — don't THROW them away.

Renew equipment and furnishings only when they are worn out, not for mere whims.

☆ Avoid gadgetry, especially in the home. Most of it makes more, not less, work — and consumes vast quantities of energy and finite resources.

☆ Make or grow whatever possible. A self-made pot or table should be a source of considerably greater pride than one that is bought — any fool with money can go and buy other people's art and imagination. Make full use of greenhouses, gardens and window boxes to grow as much edible produce as possible. Home-grown vegetables, fruit and herbs, if grown organically, are considerably healthier than their forced, fertilizer-fed, insecticide-sprayed, artificially-coloured and denatured supermarket counterparts. Exchange home-grown (home-made, home-painted, home-sculpted etc. etc.) goods with friends and neighbours to avoid waste and increase variety.

☆ Cut down waste by buying returnable bottles or using bottle banks. Don't buy goods that have been over-packaged and refuse bags wherever possible. Use re-cycled goods and re-use envelopes by using stickers.

☆ One house is enough for anybody. One car per household is MORE than enough. Use public transport whenever possible and get rid of the holiday home.

E. **Activate, educate, organise** . . .

Anybody who wants to be 'involved' can find a hundred and one different ways of doing it, whatever suits the individual concerned. Most obviously you could join/support CND, The Animal Rights Campaign, The Women's Movement, NCCL, Greenpeace, Amnesty International, The Conservationists, Greenham . . . or any other of the established protest groups and splinter groups thereof.

Alternatively (or in addition) you could be more ambitious and start the new political party. In my opinion, however, singly the most important thing that anybody could do who has a flair for organization, is sick of being unemployed/used as cheap labour and/or who believes in the possibility of a self-reliant self-sufficient nation, would be to get together with like minded people in similar positions and set up — or help OTHERS to set up — co-operatives. Individually co-operatives have obvious advantages for the operators — who reap the benefits equally in place of putting the major part of the profit from their labour into the hands of a minority — but *COLLECTIVELY* they could be a powerful force for changing the whole structure of our present society. I appeal, therefore, to those amongst the young, the unemployed and the left who are willing to give it a try to get together and organize the beginnings of an infra-structure of inter-related, inter-dependent workshops and retail outlets to manufacture and sell home[1] grown and home[1] produced goods made with British raw materials, and to provide such services to the community as building, decorating and electrical skills. I hesitate to attempt to set down a blueprint for such a venture, but to all those with imagination the possibilities are endless for diversifying into such things as co-operative building societies, banks and organic farming; for providing community housing complexes with built-in nurseries and other facilities for the community care of children and shared responsibilities in the home; for opening up a wealth of possibilities for a

1. *British*

future that a large percentage of women, blacks, the young and the unemployed would not otherwise have; and for taking the monopoly of work-opportunities, housing and food production away from government and big business and putting it where it belongs — into the hands of the people. Isolated co-operative ventures are useful, to be sure, but to have any real impact they must be collectively organized so that all excess profits (i.e. anything that is over after the whole of the workforce has been paid a pre-determined salary) can be used towards expanding the movement and providing housing for the members.

What I propose, in essence, is the inception of a grass-roots movement that is not involved, via established banks and trans-national businesses, in such exploitative investments as South African diamond mines and Indian tea plantations, and which can eventually subsist without recourse to any of the systems of exploitation euphemistically called "economics". I propose the beginnings of a society whose aims are co-operatively to care for its own — its own sick, its own disabled, its own feeble and aged, its own weak, its own distressed — without reliance on magnanimous 'hand-outs' from the rich to provide its members with pensions and benefits that have been gained at the expense of other people's labour, peace of mind, self-reliance . . . and even lives. I propose that the aims of the movement should not be to grasp, grab, consume and compete but to share, care, subsist and co-operate and that its priorities should be centred around spiritual, artistic and autonomous development. I propose that this collective co-operative movement be a limb of the existing structure for only so long as it takes to become totally independent of it, and I suggest that as it expands and recruits, it will begin to sound the death knell for the cornball culture and all the evils it represents. These proposals may terrify, horrify, excite or bemuse, but for anybody who really CARES I believe they constitute the only lasting solution for our poor, sick world — and that the time for such concerted, organized action is long, long overdue.

Nobody appreciates better than I do how difficult it is to change the habits of half a lifetime (which is why it is of PARAMOUNT importance not to teach children bad habits in the first place) and there are bound to be times when the pressure to revert to old habits will prove too much — others when the need just to BELONG will make you do and say things that your conscience will tell you were a mistake. Also, since we all have to survive within a capitalist framework it is virtually impossible to follow the rules to the letter. The attempt to subsist without recourse to foreign produce or animal protein throws up the obvious paradox that since we rely so heavily on animal produce for our food and since most of our agriculture is geared to animal production it is virtually impossible to get a reasonable, varied protein balance without using imported grains and pulses. These, however, must be viewed as intermediary hiccoughs and should not present an excuse to do NOTHING just because everything cannot, at the moment, work exactly the way we might want it to. Nothing will change overnight — it will take perseverance, hard work, patience and (initially) sacrifice — but anything that the individual can contribute is a whole lot better than nothing and the more people who are involved the quicker we will begin to see results.

Why, I hear the cornball snarling, should I bother *my*self with changing my habits? What has the state of the world got to do with *my* actions? Why should *I* care? What's in it for *ME*? Well I'm sorry if I haven't made that clear throughout the book, but for the benefit of the cornball I will reiterate.

☆ At least 450 million of the world's inhabitants suffer from malnutrition and hunger. (Almost entirely attributable to world economics.)

☆ It is estimated that the aristocracy own 18 million acres of land and 200 titled families, even after death duties, have still managed to retain estates of 500 acres or more — often considerably more. Thousands of families in Britain are homeless and destitute. Many more live in one room. Children and teenagers regularly prostitute themselves for a bed for the night. Thousands live in high-rise hells because there's not enough land for gardens.

☆ Three and a half million people are registered unemployed in this country alone (even AFTER the manipulation of the figures). The number does not include a large proportion of women doing unpaid work; it does not include the ever-increasing numbers of people locked away from 'decent' society in prisons; it does not include those in mental institutions or those dying before their time from industry-related diseases; it does not include all those on useless, compulsory 'training' schemes; it does not include anybody under the age of 16 (who are automatic 'dependants' with no individual rights and no legal means of obtaining independence).

☆ In excess of three million experiments are carried out annually in the UK on sentient and defenceless animals. Disgusting sports such as hare coursing, fox-hunting and badger-baiting — in all of which the animals involved are frequently torn apart and ALWAYS die in abject terror — are still very much a part of our 'civilized' society. Factory farming becomes ever more heartless with every opportunity to make an extra buck . . . or pound . . . or franc.

☆ Over the next five decades around two million species of plants and animals will be lost to us forever with the relentless destruction of the world's rain forests in the pursuit of profits. We live in constant danger of destroying the whole fabric of the earth — and with it our own means of survival — in the interests of providing a few with vast wealth and the many with a deluge of consumer rubbish we could all live very well without.

☆ Every year an ever-increasing number of people find they cannot cope with life as it is and fall victim to drugs in the form of pills, heroin, alcohol, glue-sniffing and tobacco. Every year thousands upon thousands die from cancers and other degenerative diseases that could be avoided. Every year the harmful effects of powerful drugs become more and more apparent as ever greater numbers of doctor-prescribed drug casualties fill up hospital beds and mental institutions. Every year old people die cold, hungry and alone.

☆ Yearly, monthly — almost daily — our freedoms are eroded as we move inexorably towards a world dominated by the demands of the market place; towards a dog-eat-dog world of corporate industrial power, puppet dictators, cheap labour and oppression; towards a world without a soul and a world without pity.

☆ The quality of our lives deteriorates with every passing decade. Individual competition makes us hostile and insecure and destroys community spirit. The private car destroys and pollutes our environment.

Boring, stressful and unhealthy jobs destroy our peace of mind and damage our health.

Divisions of race, class and gender destroy our self-confidence, fragment our needs and leave most of us, for one reason or another, resentful, lonely and confused.

The threat of violence in an increasingly heartless and unequal society is becoming a growing threat to our peace of mind and freedom of movement . . .

. . . and over it all, like the death-card of final retribution for man's insufferable arrogance, hovers the terrible spectre of nuclear war.

It is a cruel, unequal and dangerous world we live in and it is the responsibility of each and every one of us to do something to change it — before it is too late. Anybody who does *NOTHING* truly deserves the name "cornball" and should be duly ashamed of having earned it.

END

AFTERWORD

On reflection, it is obvious that much of what I have said will be misconstrued, either intentionally or otherwise, so I feel I owe it, both to myself and to my readers, to try to minimise unnecessary confusion by explaining my use of various words and phrases and by clarifying my own stance in a few of the areas most obviously open to mixed interpretation.

1. Class

I'm not particularly keen on using expressions such as working and middle class because the word "class" is loaded with socially constructed assertions of superior and inferior status with which I strongly disagree. It is undeniable, however, that different social factions DO exist, that they ARE characterised by certain attitudes and behaviour patterns and that the distinctions between them DO broadly correspond to differences in financial circumstances and background. The point that I have tried to make throughout is that the distinctions that exist are largely kept alive by the attitudes of those who are trapped inside the delineations. I do not 'class' myself in such a way precisely because I know that to do so would confine me to a narrow pattern of thought and behaviour considered 'acceptable' to my peer group and I have no desire to be so confined.[1] To be 'working class' is to know your place and stay in it, listen to the Queen's speech at Christmas and respect your betters. I do not consider myself working class. To be middle class is to be an owner-occupier, be refined of speech and behaviour, know definitively which wine goes with what at what temperature and have lunch when the working class have dinner. Whereas I confess to

1. *Which is not to lose sight of the limitations imposed upon me externally by others on account of my background, sex, financial circumstances and political outlook.*

being an owner-occupier, I do not consider myself middle class. To be upper class is to be propertied, rich and 'well' connected, despise the lower orders and say hayse and grayse in place of house and grouse. I most certainly do not fit into THAT category. I am therefore a misfit by society's definitions of social 'normality', since I am classless. This happy state of classlessness is a condition in which I believe a growing number of people now find themselves and it is not these people that I speak about when I refer to class stereotypes like Pete and Jean, but about the cornballs who keep alive the whole ridiculous idea that such rigid social delineations should be recognised. Emphatically, I cast no aspersions on the Pete's of our society for their lowly positions and paltry incomes but for their lack of perception and tunnel-visioned rigidity of outlook — and this is just as true of cornball stereotypes of *ALL* income-related classes, not just those at the bottom end of the scale.

A crucial factor in eliminating divisions in society is, without a doubt, the elimination of systems which allow minorities to assume power over the rest of the community, but the whole concept of 'classes' denoting superior and inferior categories of worth will never be expunged until cornball stereotypes from all backgrounds extricate themselves from the suffocating restrictions of class tyranny and begin to act as free-thinking individuals with the power to determine their own destiny — and thus to experience the rich potential of human interaction to the full.

2. God

My own understanding of 'God', I should make it clear (if I haven't already), bears no resemblance to the one pushed by preachers of the Jewish and Christian faiths. I do not see God as an external, authoritative figure but as an integral part of everything that keeps the universe together. Whether an omnipotent being exists or not seems to me to be immaterial when it comes to deciding how we should conduct our lives, since the results of our actions will be the same whichever is the case. We do not need a paternalistic figure of authority to rap our knuckles for our mis-deeds, because retribution is built in to our actions by dint of our very relationship with each other and with the forces of Nature. Figures like Scrooge who place too much value on material wealth are invariably punished by their own loneliness and paucity of spirit. Those who give nothing of themselves receive nothing of others in return. Those who exploit and mistreat their fellow beings become mean-spirited, greedy and insecure, through fear of being treated in the same way themselves. Humankind constantly reaps retribution in ill-health through greed, sloth, selfishness and imprudence. God is, if not omnipotent, omnipresent. God is love, our conscience, our spirit and the very essence of our being: God is intricately woven into the immutable laws of Nature and the cosmos: God is the ubiquitous and inescapable spectre of self-loathing.

Whatever the source of the dynamics of our existence may be, the power it holds over us remains the same and whether or not we choose to dress it in trousers and pay weekly homage to it makes no difference to the retribution it is capable of visiting upon arrogant humankind, nor do such obsequious exhibitions of 'faith' excuse any of us our individual responsibility to order our lives in acknowledgement of its existence.

3. Individual Autonomy

Individual autonomy is the ability of individuals to survive without subservience to outside, authoritative bodies of power (such as Government, Police and Army) and without dependence upon Government-created institutions such as compulsory schooling, the judiciary, 'orthodox' medicine, and neatly packaged religious 'beliefs'. Education, health and spiritual and moral development are (should be) matters of personal choice and responsibility, not the exclusive domain of institutions with rigid rules, pre-determined guidelines and convenient priorities. "Education" within an institutionalised framework has as little to do with real learning as "medicine" has to do with healthy living, as "law and order" with genuine, social responsibility or "religious faith" with any true, personal commitment to a philosophy. Individuals cannot 'live and learn' if they are constantly told how to live and what to learn.

I should make it abundantly clear that individual autonomy is not the same thing as right-wing "individualism", which is built around the totally selfish pursuit of personal goals and encompasses a complete disregard for the effects on other people, other animals and the environment. The rugged, right-wing individualism of one person is dependent upon the subjugation and subsequent loss of freedom of ninety-nine others. Conversely, individual autonomy does not rule out social co-operation and interaction, nor does it absolve the individual from responsibility to the community. Properly organised by a responsible public, individual autonomy can exist in functional harmony with socialist ideals of equal access to knowledge, equitable distribution of goods and equal rights to necessary services. The stumbling blocks to the successful marriage between individual autonomy, equality and community co-operation are, as I have pointed out in the text, a) the adherence to socially-constructed 'masculine' values as the yardstick of human excellence, and the subsequent subjugation of women, b) the existence of a centralised power structure operated by and for a minority, and c) a world-wide obsession with constant, material growth. Until the desirability of all these factors is discredited, neither equality nor individual freedom will ever be realised and community co-operation will be doomed to failure. This does not mean, however, that the whole concept of such a marriage is either unworkable or unrealistic — merely that it requires determined effort to achieve.

4. National Autonomy

The ability to survive as a nation without recourse to foreign powers for 'protection'. Dependence leads as inexorably to subjugation on a national as it does on a personal level.

5. National self-sufficiency

The ability to feed, clothe and house the whole nation

and provide it with sufficient energy to supply it with heat and power without dependence upon, or exploitation of, other peoples, lands and resources, coupled with freedom from the exploitation of our own labour by foreign, multi-national interests.

6. National Autonomy and Nationalism

I can well see in advance that my proposals for "National Autonomy and self-sufficiency" will excite the shock-horror ringing of alarm bells in the minds of 'internationalists' and I shall no doubt be accused of preaching rampant jingoism and exciting the masses to new peaks of nationalistic fervour. This I see as an unnecessary fear in view of all the other measures I advocate simultaneously. I suppose I sound defensive, but since what some may see as mere chauvinism-in-sheep's-clothing forms a substantial part of my proposals for revolutionary change, I feel I must try to eliminate as many of the reasons as possible for its out-of-hand dismissal.

In order to see national autonomy in its true perspective it has to be viewed in the context of the 20th century and with full consideration of the role played by super-power interventionism and conglomerate business interests throughout the world. Do we, for example, see Nicaragua's efforts to free itself from American non-colonial 'investments' as unacceptable "nationalism" and can we really condemn their national pride as chauvinism in the same breath as we might condemn Hitler's Germany? The two seem to me to be worlds apart, and for one very obvious reason — Nicaragua is trying to defend itself from the aggression of another power, whereas Germany was itself the aggressor. It is arguable that today's national pride used as a defence mechanism can in its turn become tomorrow's aggression, but this must realistically be seen as extremely unlikely (if not downright ridiculous) in view of the inordinate power of the U.S.A.

National pride in autonomy and self-sufficiency is a whole different ball-game from jingoistic, empire-building, national aggression towards other peoples. I am not advocating a new "Great" Britain built on the old

---

| **Errata** |
| American non-colonial should read American neo-colonial |

obsessions of expansionism, wealth-creation and colonialism but a new nation with new priorities and a new kind of pride — a pride in its independence, a pride in the equality of its people and a pride in its responsible and compassionate attitude towards *other* peoples. What I am advocating is not a nation seeking new heights of irresponsible selfishness and rapacious greed but a responsible, caring nation of responsible caring people that will never again be a threat to other peoples or a parasitic drain on their resources and who at the same time will be free, both individually and nationally, from subjugation by external bodies of power.

7. Nature

It is not difficult to envisage that those of a mind to will interpret my desire to see the marrying of God and Nature as nothing short of giving capitalism the blessing of God by seemingly condoning such "natural" concepts as dog-eat-dog aggression and the survival of the fittest. This, however, is neither my intention nor my belief, as I think I have made abundantly clear in everything else I have said. Such behaviour may have been "natural" at the outset of our evolution since our survival depended upon fighting off threats from other species, but territorial aggression and contentious behaviour today not only cause us nothing but problems, they actually THREATEN our survival. It does not seem sensible to me, therefore, to consider such behaviour as natural or desirable. In most cases, my use of the word "Nature" can be taken in its wider context, encompassing the phenomena of growth and reproduction and the interaction between plants, animals, the atmosphere and the cosmos. Where it is used in the more specific context of 'human' nature it is used in an adaptive rather than a rigid capacity and is not deemed to be subject to the same immutable laws as "NATURE" used in its wider context, i.e. Human Nature may have to adapt and evolve in order to conform to the immutable laws governing our survival. Since God and natural phenomena are inseparable, human beings must be in harmony with both in order to reconcile their nature with their spirit — and hence with their survival. If we allow our nature to threaten our survival, we have lost touch with God. If we pretend that God can be separated from our bodies, our sexual desires and the whole wonder of Nature's creation then we make a mockery of ourselves — and of God.

Wealth *v* Christianity

Finally, my attack upon the hypocrisy of aristocratic Henry's quasi-Christian conscience and its dangerous and divisive effects upon society could quite easily be interpreted as an attack upon Christianity itself, but this was not my intention. Whereas I do not believe Jesus Christ to have been (in a literal sense) 'the Son of God', (and certainly not of the misogynistic God of the Old Testament) nonetheless I have no quarrel with Christ the humanitarian philosopher, Christ the spiritual redeemer, Christ the voice of the meek and oppressed and Christ the bleeding heart of humanity. My quarrel is not with Christ but with Henry and his manipulation of the Christian doctrine to excuse his own moral defects and to suit his own selfish ends. Palpably, the source of Henry's moral downfall does not rest with women, sex and communism, as he tries so desperately hard to convince himself, but with his own greed, his own power-lust, his own selfishness and his own unwillingness to open his heart to his fellow beings. The pursuit, or acquisition of vast wealth (or property) and the worship of such false idols as 'market forces' run in direct opposition to spiritual development and moral responsibility and the fact that conscience-ridden, noblesse oblige, aristocratic Henries are now gradually being superseded by secular, hard-nosed, plutocratic Thatcherites does not mean that spiritual needs and moral guilt have miraculously disappeared. The same old anomalies have still to be resolved and if the new, opportunist, Henries — the brash merchants and ruthless industrialists, the sharp speculators and puppet politicians — cannot find the courage to own up to the morally unacceptable nature of their ambitions and activities, then a new generation of innocents will inevitably have to suffer in order to shoulder their guilt. How this will be manifested is a question for speculation, but I suspect it will move further and further along well-worn paths of prejudice and bigotry — complete with political witch-hunts, fanatical religious sects obsessed with the evils of sex, persecution of women and all extra-establishment groups and 'hang-'em-high' moral outrage. (Maybe even U.S.A.-style vigilanteism). There is no doubt in my mind that such reactionary behaviour, along with 1985-style plutocrats, aristocrats and right-wing moralists, would be treated by Jesus Christ — in equal proportion — to the same contempt as were the rich, the money-lenders and the hypocrites of his own time.

POST SCRIPT

I said I wasn't prepared to set down a blueprint for the 'New Society' in the body of the book but I would, nevertheless (as an afterthought) like merely to make a few points and moot a few suggestions as to how such a society might progress — if only to make clear my own vision of hope for the future.

☆ The movement would need an injection of finance at its outset, which could quite possibly be raised by means of benefits and rock concerts given by sympathetic performers. It would benefit greatly from having the backing of all the various 'alternative' factions and from the willingness of existing co-operatives and organisations to join it. The movement would have to have an 'organisational body' in order to give it cohesion, but the members of this body would not be afforded privileges, would not have any 'authority' and would frequently fluctuate.

☆ The profit motive would have to be employed at the inception of the movement, and probably for quite some considerable time, but the ultimate aim would be its abolition. All 'profit' and 'investment' would, however, be used solely for the expansion of the movement and there would be no profit-sharing scheme. One of the main aims of the movement would be to shift emphasis away from the present obsession with individual material advancement and away from dependence on the 'reward' system.

☆ There would be no division of labour within the movement, no differentials, no bonus schemes and no trades unions. It would be advisable for all the members to learn a variety of skills in order not to become hidebound in a particular job — although anybody who was happy to do this would be allowed to do so. It should be possible to employ mentally sub-normal people to do simple, repetitive work, which would be mutually beneficial (although I envisage this may initially incite some shock-horror displays of hypocrisy from the cornball element).

☆ Given the reality of our finite resources and of the necessity to take a responsible attitude towards the conservation of the environment it is obvious that '*every*body cannot have *every*thing'. Also, not only is industrial mass production irresponsible and environmentally undesirable, it also becomes counter-productive in terms of social benefits (e.g. *Every*body owning a car to increase their freedom of movement means that *every*body, eventually, ends up in the same traffic jam). This means that, given the fact that the 'New Society' will not be based upon the present system of inequality in which *some* people have absolutely everything and others have absolutely nothing, the movement would have to devise a means of ensuring an element of individual choice for the acquisition of a limited number of 'luxury' items, and to determine where necessity ends and luxury begins on the basis of available resources and points of counter-productivity. This could be achieved with the joint use of free amenities and work tickets. For example, the members of the movement could (eventually) be given free housing and a pre-determined amount of free food, heating and clothing. Beyond this they could be issued work tickets on which they would have recorded 'credits' and these credits would be crossed off in exchange for desired commodities. Since everybody would have the same number of credits it would be quite easy to detect any frauds merely by observing the number of acquisitions in any one person's possession. The 'price' of such goods would be determined by availability of the resources necessary to produce them. Raw materials for individual artistic pursuits would have to be acquired in the same way, and everything possible would have to be shared. Equipment such as stereo units, musical instruments, cookers, washing machines, etc. would all have be used communally.

☆ Housing complexes built or acquired by the movement would be constructed on the assumptions that:—

a) Everybody should be allowed the opportunity to live independently if they wished to and should not be made dependent, financially or spatially, upon family units (this would apply to children as well as adults). This would require provision of individual units for all members of the complex and space to expand to accommodate new additions. Anybody wishing to live as a couple, or family, would be free to do so as long as all the participants agreed to do so.

b) Everybody should be allowed a degree of privacy and the space for autonomous, artistic development.

c) People deserve to live in pollution-free environments and peaceful surroundings, preferably amidst Nature's bountiful gifts of flora and fauna. Space would therefore be provided for such surroundings, either in the form of individual or communal gardens — or a mixture of the two. This would also give youngsters the freedom to play unfettered and in safety. The only vehicles owned by the movement would be trade vehicles and private locomotion would by public transport, push-bike — and perhaps by shared use of low-energy consumption vehicles like the Sinclair trike. (Exceptions to this rule would have to be made for the disabled.)

☆ Children are not a separate species, they are just small, inexperienced people. They should therefore be treated with the same respect afforded to adults and given the credit for being able to acquire knowledge in the same way as the rest of the community. Young people would therefore be taught to read, write and do simple arithmetic, after which they would be left to learn and develop within the community and to share responsibility for their own welfare and for that of the community. 'School' would be the community itself and specialised higher education would take place in the shared company of adults, not be specifically and exclusively designed for a particular age group.

☆ People need to develop and exercise their artistic skill, both individually and collectively. Every possible provision would therefore be made for acquiring skills and for participating in community projects like theatrical productions, concerts, carnivals, gymnastic displays, pantomime, ice spectaculars, etc. etc.

☆ Sport is good for the body and a limited amount of team competition would perhaps be no bad thing in the context of an otherwise co-operative community. Village-green-style cricket, netball, football and rounders matches could usefully be supported by the movement as a source of entertainment and exercise for its members, provided there was no discrimination and providing it did not become part of any wider competitive network . . . .

. . . . and so on.